DRUG TESTING
EXPOSED

DRUG TESTING
EXPOSED

LOOPHOLES & TRADE SECRETS:

How Businesses, Federal & State
Agencies, Law Enforcement, Users &
Rehabilitation Profit from Them

by

MICHAEL A. BONVENTRE

Printed by Createspace

First Printing: fill in date, 2011

ISBN: 1463661142
ISBN-13: 9781463661144
LCCN: 2011911147

Printed in the United States of America

CONTENTS

ACKNOWLEDGEMENTS

To my family of proud Italian-American heritage I express my deepest appreciation. I am grateful for having had the experience of growing up in a family of manual laborers and shoe factory workers. They were hardworking people whose work ethic, high moral principles and deeply ingrained decency were shining examples. Their standards gave me the ability to fight all the evils they stood against.

To all my childhood friends, acquaintances and relatives who unfortunately chose to be drawn into lives of drugs and crime and who now struggle through adulthood with no real goal in life or are suffering the health consequences of past years of substance abuse and especially to those who did not survive.

To the law enforcement officers and professionals in Florida, and across the country, who, during my three deep undercover years, treated me as one of their own, I give my deepest respect and gratitude. These public servants are true Americans, who took personal risks for a civilian who was going into uncharted territory fighting crime and drugs and often ignoring convention and protocol.

To Mike Levine one of the nation's most highly decorated former DEA agents, who served a thirty five year career as an international federal narcotics officer, trial consultant, expert witness, and bestselling author of books exposing the failed war on drugs for befriending me, supporting my endeavors and repeatedly allowing me to be a guest on his *Expert Witness* radio show. In 2006, he honored me in a republication of his book *Fight Back by acknowledging* my efforts as "waging one of the most hopeful FIGHT BACK wars since the plan was first published." You have my deepest gratitude and utmost respect.

To Agent Mark P., My journey into fighting and exposing corruption started in 1982 when one of your colleagues dismissed my family as collateral damage. From the time we met in 1986, your efforts and involvement redeemed your agency in my eyes. Thanks for bringing dignity back to the Binghamton FBI.

To L.G. Space, author and one of my closest friends, confidant and supporter. Thanks for raising your cholesterol over a thousand breakfasts while we discussed, rehashed and talked about this project and so much more. I truly appreciate you.

To Jocelyn T. Bailey for her outstanding cover concept.

To Richard R. Dilworth, for introducing me to *Fight Back*, your persistence in promoting my efforts in fighting drugs in our community and introducing me to influential people throughout the U.S.

To Mary Pat Hyland[3], author, friend and confidant. Your support and guidance are much appreciated.

To Suzanne Meredith, author and friend. Thank you for initiating the idea that evolved into this book.

To my nieces and nephew, Jocelyn, Lauren and Andrew, I couldn't be more proud of you. You are proof that proper parenting and close family help kids make the right choices even when surrounded by drugs in school.

To Deb Lovas, Warren/Youngstown, Ohio, the bravest most energetic one-woman army I have ever had the pleasure of working with. My undying respect, she is Grandma hear her roar.☺

To Amber Olmstead, one of the most valuable people in the Rapid Drug Test Systems family. Thank you for the outstanding work ethic, commitment and genuine enthusiasm you bring to work. You exemplify the RDTS philosophy and I feel blessed to consider you, your children and family as an extension of my own.

A special thanks to the countless citizens, clients, business owners, acquaintances, anonymous public servants and law enforcers who shared their most intimate, personal and professional stories that motivate me to continue the fight.

To Ladylaw Publishing, LLC for working with me and guiding me through this project from its inception. The research, guidance and collaboration in helping me translate my personal and professional experiences, into a finished product were superb and invaluable. I would recommend any first-time author to you.

To my wife, Jo A. Fabrizio, a proper acknowledgment would become another full-length book. So let me humbly thank you for twenty two years of selfless unconditional love, understanding, and support of who I am.

INTRODUCTION

I have committed myself to educating people and businesses about the effects of drug users, drug dealers and drug gangs since 1982.

My journey began when my family's business was extorted by organized crime and then further victimized by law enforcement agencies that prioritized their budgets and personal agendas with complete disregard for our concerns and safety.

This prompted me to become a citizen crime fighter working with federal, state and county law enforcement agencies throughout the nation. Working with law enforcement for three years as a deep undercover organized crime and narcotics consultant, and having overseen more than one hundred million dollars in extortion and drug traffic sales, gave me an exclusive look at how drugs influence businesses, families and communities at every level. I saw, firsthand, how the long reaching effects of bureaucracy, misguided law enforcement agendas, politics and gangs touch every part of our daily existence.

This experience ignited a passion in me to expose the faults, inconsistencies and loopholes in the entire drug industry from law enforcement to testing, prevention and rehabilitation.

I will never forget my first encounter with an FBI agent who proclaimed, my family was "acceptable collateral damage" in his agency's agenda to continue a twenty five-year investigation of the criminals that embezzled my family and were threatening our lives.

I can't forget the face of the man who could not believe his business associates helped addict his daughters so they could control and manipulate them to rob and steal.

There was also the district manager of a grocery store chain who refused to acknowledge that his stores were being robbed by drug addicted employees on a regular basis.

Then we have the CEO of a major corporation who did not want to hear that the vice president of the company was draining the corporation of hundreds of thousands of dollars in materials and labor in return for the fulfillment of his personal vices.

I could go on but the point is clear apathy, sticking your head in the sand and living in denial do not solve anything. A drug testing program that follows the rules and is run with integrity and law enforcement agendas that serve citizens rather than criminals, budgets and job security could prevent much of this.

Without realizing it, the incidents from 1982 to 1999 shaped my destiny. They influenced my next step to get inside the very industry designed to control and eliminate drugs in the workplace. With this goal in mind, I was instrumental in forming Rapid Drug Test Systems, a business which is nationally recognized for raising the standards in drug testing, training and consulting. I am the operations manager and senior train the trainer of this company. For those unfamiliar with the industry, a train the trainer is an advanced certification that allows an individual to return back to their company to become an in-house trainer. Through training and consulting, I bring awareness to drug test collectors, business owners, human resource professionals, parents and concerned individuals. Through testing, I implement the rules and regulations which are designed to keep drugs out of the workplace. Or so I thought.

The deeper I delve into the drug industry, the stronger my passion becomes to tell anyone who will listen why truly compliant drug testing and prevention are the ultimate obstacle to law enforcement, human resource professionals and community leaders. Throughout this book, you will read personal, firsthand accounts of why drug testing and prevention are failing at every level. You will read my opinion of what the problems are and what the solutions could be.

So, why should you read this book? Well, if you own or are responsible for operating a business you will learn how having a less than fully compliant drug testing program actually hurts your business and the benefits a compliant program will produce. Concerned citizens will learn how law enforcement and politics thrive at your expense.

Likewise, families need to be concerned about the failures of the drug testing industry because it affects you on all levels, in your workplace, in your neighborhoods and in your schools. It also influences your children's experiences outside of school.

From your own experiences, each of you who read this book will bring expectations about this subject matter. May I ask that you proceed with an open mind?

If, like me, you were raised in the fifties and sixties or before you were probably taught to believe that presidents don't lie, all law enforcement professionals are above corruption and integrity is more important than a paycheck. Sadly, all you have to do is turn on the evening news and you will quickly be reminded that there is hardly anything left that is not motivated by profit, personal gain and immediate gratification. I have discussed the issues raised in this book with countless drug testing professionals, law enforcement professionals, heads of federal and state agencies, politicians, educational professionals, parents, and media in hundreds of settings. If I had a nickel for each time I heard,

"I find that hard to believe," I could be retired in a Maui beach house. What do I find hard to believe? That in this day and age anybody would find anything hard to believe! This does not make me a "conspiracy theorist" or a skeptic, it simply reflects my life experiences and my sincere desire to know, and expose, the truth, the whole truth and nothing but the truth not just what feels good, is socially acceptable. or (God forbid) politically correct.

So, reader, as you embark on this journey with me, park your pre-conceived notions and all the propaganda that the media have fed you over the years and thoughtfully consider what is being presented here. You may agree, you may disagree, but you will certainly be challenged and find much to think about.

MICHAEL J. SATZ
STATE ATTORNEY
SEVENTEENTH JUDICIAL CIRCUIT OF FLORIDA

BROWARD COUNTY COURTHOUSE
FORT LAUDERDALE, FLORIDA 33301
PHONE (305) 765 ▓▓▓▓▓▓

April 18, 1986

To Whom It May Concern:

This is to certify that Michael A. Bonventre, date of birth / /57, has been an operative, in the capacity as a source of confidential information pursuant to criminal investigations being conducted by law enforcement agencies in the State of Florida.

Mr. Bonventre has been acting in this capacity from the Summer of 1983 to December 1985.

For law enforcement purposes only and further clarification of the capacity that Mr. Bonventre worked in, please contact Investigator ▓▓▓▓▓▓▓▓▓▓▓ or Investigator ▓▓▓▓▓▓▓▓ at ▓▓▓▓▓▓

Sincerely,

▓▓▓▓▓▓▓▓▓▓

▓▓▓▓▓▓▓▓

Judicial Investigator
Seventeenth Judicial Circuit
State of Florida

▓/▓

I continued to work with NY law enforcement agencies on a limited basis while restarting my private life until the indictments were handed out between 1987 &1988. The trials began in 1989.

THE FEDERAL DRUG AND ALCOHOL TESTING INDUSTRY

Overview

The Omnibus Transportation Employee Testing Act of 1991[1] requires the drug and alcohol testing of U.S. Department of Transportation applicants and employees. The (DOT) requires that all the agencies under its regulation have policies in place that fully explain who must conduct the tests, and how and when they are to be conducted. [2] In addition, those policies must be made accessible to all parties affected under the program.

History

The Omnibus Transportation Employee Testing Act of 1991 resulted from congressional hearings which were prompted by accidents involving drug and alcohol use in railroads, aviation, trucking and other modes of transportation.[3] Citing public safety as its goal, Congress presented several accidents as its motivation to act. On January 4, 1987, an accident occurred in Chase, Maryland between an Amtrak passenger train and a Conrail freight train. The Conrail train's engineer and brakeman testified that they had been smoking marijuana in the train prior to the accident. The NTSB (National Transportation Safety Board) found that a probable cause of the accident was the engineer's failure as a result of impairment from the use of marijuana. In addition, the brakeman tested positive for PCP in his urine. This accident killed 16 people and injured 170 others. [4]

The hearings uncovered the link between accidents and the use of drugs and alcohol. The record contains examples of many accidents involving trains, planes, trucks and other common carriers.

The legislation initially only introduced a requirement for the alcohol testing of DOT employees, but grew to include an expanded list of drugs for which tests would be conducted before being finalized.

Who Is Covered

According to the U.S. Department of Transportation and outlined in the *Code of Federal Regulations*, any employee performing safety-sensitive transportation functions, including ones in the aviation, trucking, railroads, mass transit, and pipelines industries are required to be tested. [5] Each industry has its own definition of duties deemed safety sensitive, but the term generally describes a position in which an alcohol or drug impairment constitutes a direct threat to public safety. Essentially, any employee performing operations in a commercial capacity is subject to testing.

Testing Procedures

All DOT agencies have the option to administer the program internally, or outsource some or all of the program's functions. No matter the option chosen, drug testing is usually conducted via urinalysis, and alcohol testing is conducted with the assistance of a breath testing or saliva collection device. The entire process begins with the collector, who will be discussed in a later section of this book. The results are then reviewed by either a medical review officer or breath alcohol technician, who attests to the accuracy of the drug testing process.

For a valid urine test, the following steps are taken:

Subpart E - Urine Specimen Collections

§ 40.63 What steps does the collector take in the collection process before the employee provides a urine specimen?

As the collector, you must take the following steps before the employee provides the urine specimen:

(a) Complete Step 1 of the CCF.

(b) Instruct the employee to wash and dry his or her hands at this time. You must tell the employee not to wash his or her hands again until after delivering the specimen to you. You must not give the employee any further access to water or other materials that could be used to adulterate or dilute a specimen.

(c) Select, or allow the employee to select, an individually wrapped or sealed collection container from collection kit materials. Either you or the employee, with both of you present, must unwrap or break the seal of the collection container. You must not unwrap or break the seal on any specimen bottle at this time. You must not allow the employee to take anything from the collection kit into the room used for urination except the collection container.

(d) Direct the employee to go into the room used for urination, provide a specimen of at least 45 mL, not flush the toilet, and return to you with the specimen as soon as the employee has completed the void.

(1) Except in the case of an observed or a monitored collection (see §§40.67 and 40.69), neither

you nor anyone else may go into the room with the employee.

(2) As the collector, you may set a reasonable time limit for voiding.

(e) You must pay careful attention to the employee during the entire collection process to note any conduct that clearly indicates an attempt to tamper with a specimen (e.g., substitute urine in plain view or an attempt to bring into the collection site an adulterant or urine substitute). If you detect such conduct, you must require that a collection take place immediately under direct observation (see §40.67) and complete Step 2 by noting the conduct in the "Remarks" line of the CCF and the fact that the collection was observed by checking the "Observed" box. You must also, as soon as possible, inform the DER and collection site supervisor that a collection took place under direct observation and the reason for doing so.

[65 FR 79526, Dec.19, 2000, as amended at 75 FR 59107, September 27, 2010]

For a valid alcohol test, the following steps are taken:

Subpart K - Testing Sites, Forms, Equipment and Supplies Used in Alcohol Testing

§ 40.223   What steps must be taken to protect the security of alcohol testing sites?

(a) If you are a BAT, STT, or other person operating an alcohol testing site, you must prevent unauthorized personnel from entering the testing site.

(1) The only people you are to treat as authorized persons are employees being tested, BATs, STTs, and other alcohol testing site workers, DERs, employee representatives authorized by the employer (e.g., on the basis of employer policy or labor-management agreement), and DOT agency representatives.

(2) You must ensure that all persons are under the supervision of a BAT or STT at all times when permitted into the site.

(3) You may remove any person who obstructs, interferes with, or causes unnecessary delay in the testing process.

(b) As the BAT or STT, you must not allow any person other than you, the employee, or a DOT agency representative to actually witness the testing process (see §§40.241–40.255).

(c) If you are operating an alcohol testing site, you must ensure that when an EBT or ASD is not being used for testing, you store it in a secure place.

(d) If you are operating an alcohol testing site, you must ensure that no one other than BATs or other employees of the site have access to the site when an EBT is unsecured.

(e) As a BAT or STT, to avoid distraction that could compromise security, you are limited to conducting an alcohol test for only one employee at a time.

(1) When an EBT screening test on an employee indicates an alcohol concentration of 0.02 or higher, and the same EBT will be used for the confirmation test, you are not allowed to use the EBT for a test on another employee before completing the confirmation test on the first employee.

(2) As a BAT who will conduct both the screening and the confirmation test, you are to complete the entire screening and confirmation process on one employee before starting the screening process on another employee.

(3) You are not allowed to leave the alcohol testing site while the testing process for a given employee is in progress, except to notify a supervisor or contact a DER for assistance in the case an employee or other person who obstructs, interferes with, or unnecessarily delays the testing process.

Time Frame

The Omnibus Transportation Employee Testing Act of 1991 mandates that testing occur pre-employment, in the event of reasonable suspicion, post-accident, return to duty and follow up, and at predetermined random rates. [6] The rates set for testing vary by industry, with most rates set at an annual requirement of ten percent of employees tested for alcohol, and ranges between twenty-five to fifty percent for drug testing.

Consequences

The DOT requires that employees who test positive for restricted substances or refuse a test be immediately removed from safety-sensitive functions. [7] An additional requirement is that offending employees be given a list of qualified substance abuse programs, with the decision of who pays for the services left up to the employer's discretion. Although the DOT does not have uniform rules in place regarding termination or any other personnel decision, it does establish that employees wishing to return to any safety-sensitive position must complete the return to duty process as specified by their employer and substance abuse program.

THE LOOPHOLES

The very language of the *Code of Federal Regulations creates huge loopholes.* In some places, the regulations contain the words "should," "can" or "may." This allows for some discretion (otherwise known as "loopholes.") Other sections contain the word "must" which requires absolute compliance with that part of the regulation. For example, a donor must display the contents of his pockets. This is absolute. When the word must is followed by "<u>if practicable</u>" the reader is invited to manipulate the intent at will and most will do just that.

A good example of this is that part of the regulation which states that when an alcohol test is required with a drug test, the alcohol test must be done prior to the drug test, to the greatest extent practicable. [8] This allows the collector to determine what is practicable. I have had donors present themselves for drug and alcohol tests and beg to do the drug test first because they really had to go. To the untrained, improperly trained or inattentive collector it seems like a harmless request. However, the donor may have brought in urine which will cool to below acceptable temperature if the alcohol test is conducted first. Also delaying the alcohol test allows the

25

donor additional time to sober up. Ten to fifteen minutes can make the difference between positive and negative under federal guidelines.

2. FEDERAL MANDATED TESTING LOOPHOLES: FIRST: Conflict of Interest

In most businesses, the majority of drug testing is the responsibility of the human resource professional. A large part of their job is to fill jobs and keep them filled. Only then can a company operate and meet its bottom line. This places the HR professional in a conflict. They must fill jobs but have to put potential employees through the drug testing program. If these job candidates do not pass the drug test, then HR needs to find more people to fill the jobs who then have to be drug tested and on and on it goes.

I have found a common practice among HR reps is to allow job candidates excessive or extended notice prior to a test. This makes it possible for the potential employee to clean out his system. This practice is so prevalent it appears to be an unwritten trade secret among the HR world. Understand that cleaning out his system does not mean solving his drug problem. All you get is an employee who is clear of drugs on the day of his test not an employee who is drug-free. Yet another practice is for HR to return job seekers for multiple tests using multiple collection facilities until a negative test result is received. This allows them to proclaim the potential employee "drug-free."

A little known fact, still another unwritten trade secret, is that in many companies the human resource department is closely associated with public relations and/or customer service. This creates a conflict at a different level. No company wants to be known for having employees on drugs. If too many drug tests are failed, the company can "look bad." Much pressure can be brought to bear on the human resource professionals by those charged with the responsibility to create, and protect, the company's public image. So, again, the HR professional is under pressure to keep the drug test failures to a minimum.

HR is often inappropriately aligned with the medical review officer MRO. (see Glossary). HR often acts as the designated employer representative DER (see Glossary) who is caught between the collector and the MRO. The MRO provides the final analysis of the drug test results. Many times, the HR professional will be pressured to encourage the collector to look the other way on technicalities that could result in the cancellation of a drug test or neglect to report those technicalities. The MRO would be required to cancel such a test. I have frequently been "encouraged" to overlook the fact that a donor left the facility during a test. [9] This is a clear violation of the rules and reason for the cancellation of a test. [10, 11, 12, 13]

Another trade secret, and one of the most commonly used loopholes, is to put employees to work without the pre-employment drug tests. The employees are then asked to take the "pre-employment" test three to four weeks *after* they have been on the job or at least long enough for them to get clean. I have found this to be common practice to meet hiring quotas since there is no allowance for replacing pre-employment testing with post-employment testing. The donor should never be employed before the printed results of the test are actually received by the potential employer. To do otherwise thoroughly thwarts the intent of "pre-employment" testing.

Businesses can eliminate this conflict. I have assisted numerous businesses in implementing corrective measures that avoid this conflict while still allowing HR to do its job. I have been inspired by the number of HR professionals who have spoken to me "off the record" admitting that they did not agree nor approve of some of the practices they were forced to follow but in the end it fell to a choice between their integrity and their job.

SECOND: When management is not drug tested

Under federal regulations, management does not need to be tested if their positions are not considered "safety sensitive" as defined by the federal regulations and the company.[14] This gets upper management off the hook and leaves the issue of testing to their discretion. While many management positions may not be considered safety sensitive jobs the decisions management makes generally impact directly on safety issues.

Requiring tests of the rank and file, while exempting management, often causes resentment. I have seen it create an "us" vs. "them" mentality. This is especially true when workers know that their former co-worker, who is now management, used drugs or alcohol on the job. I recall one large company where many workers, whom I saw on a regular basis when performing their required random tests, complained long and loud about one certain manager who was reputed to drink large quantities of alcohol. As a drug tester, it was certainly not my position to tell upper management about the discord, resentment and ill-will this created in the rank and file, but I saw the effect the lack of respect had on the morale of these men and women.

The flip side of this policy shows itself when former co-employees, who previously drank or did drugs on the job together, now find themselves in the often uncomfortable position of manager and employee. Since managers are often promoted out of the rank and file, it is not uncommon for former fellow employees to be placed in this position. Many managers feel pressure to overlook the behavior of employees with whom they have a personal relationship.

We have to keep in mind that people do drugs. Their job titles and positions within a company do not exempt them from undermining the concept of a drug-free workplace.

Yet another outgrowth of this selective testing policy is what I call the job transfer shuffle. If a worker transfers from a safety sensitive job to a non-safety sensitive job, he or she can effectively avoid the drug test. I have seen workers give up their commercial drivers licenses (CDL) so they are not considered safety sensitive. This allows them to avoid the testing process while continuing to work in their company albeit under a different job title. I fault the companies who allow this policy thereby creating safe havens for drug users.

THIRD: Independent Contractors

It is a common practice for companies to hire independent contractors, truck drivers, plumbers, welders, manufacturing, retail etc., for certain jobs. Independent contractors are often not required to be drug tested by the company because they are not, technically, "employees" subject to the company's drug and alcohol policy. In addition, the subs are often provided through temporary agencies that may have weak or non-existent drug and alcohol testing programs.

Basically the company fills the needed position while entirely bypassing the drug testing and liability issues. In addition, independent contractors commonly alert their employees weeks and sometimes months, in advance to prepare for the drug test, if required by the contract they are bidding on.

Not long ago, the opportunity to bid on a highway rest stop roof contract brought several contractors to my office. One company had forty employees. A manager said to his employees I need eight clean drug tests to qualify us for the bidding process. Can I have eight volunteers who are confident they can pass the drug test? After the sixth consecutive failed test result, and a declining number of volunteers, the contractor decided not to bid that job. Several other roofing companies, ranging from twelve to sixty employees, could not find eight people to pass a drug test thereby eliminating them from the bid process as well.

With nearly thirty years in the industry, eleven of those being directly involved in testing, this was no surprise to me. If you identify a specific industry I can with a great degree of accuracy identify its' drug of choice and percentage of users.

FOURTH: Collector shopping

In order to implement a drug and alcohol program, the first thing a company needs to do is find a collector.[15] Shopping for the collector takes many forms. It is relatively easy for a company with one location to find a local collector. A company with larger needs, or multiple locations, finds it's not so easy and that often results in the use of the third party administrator. [16]

The third party administer is a broker, a person or company who promises to find multiple collectors at the cheapest prices. The third party administrator often bids on the contracts and then looks for the collectors to fill them. I recall one fellow who bid on state contracts that required collectors - you guessed - it all across the state. He was not, and had never been, a collector so he had limited understanding of the collection process. His only goal was to provide collectors not experienced collectors, not well-trained collectors, not properly certified collectors but simply collectors in each location required by his contract and all at the lowest possible price.

I have been asked to serve as a quality control consultant for some of the largest third party administrators (TPA's) and the companies they service. Some of these companies were looking for collectors in up to a thousand locations nationwide. Bodies, budgets and bottom lines were the focus. I soon discovered most companies basically provided lip service to the notion they wanted any "quality" control. Every recommendation about implementing basic standards for collectors or ensuring they are properly trained is almost always met with resistance and a "don't rock the boat" attitude. So long as someone responding to the title "collector" answered the ad, inquiry or phone call, the company is satisfied.

While smaller companies may not face the same issues as their larger counterparts, they still engage in collector shopping. Even though mandated to be drug tested, small employers often manipulate their random programs by giving advance notice to the employee. It is common practice to leave relatives and longtime employees who they know do drugs out of the program in the hopes of shielding them from the testing process. Many companies run two or more random programs off the books. Unlike their large counterparts, these small companies decide to choose their collectors personally. They usually opt for testing facilities that are known for not following protocol and resulting in, shall we say more "lenient" testing standards.

These loopholes are just a sample of the number of creative ways companies maneuver around drug testing requirements. Many additional examples are discussed in my trainings, seminars and consulting sessions.

3. FORENSIC/NON-MANDATED TESTING LOOPHOLES:

Before I get to the core of this section, which is loopholes that exist in non-mandated drug testing, I first need to say a word about federal -vs- non federal. There are basically two types of workplace drug testing: federally mandated which we discussed earlier and non-mandated otherwise known as non-regulated or forensic drug testing. This is perhaps the most misunderstood and misapplied area in the drug testing industry. Nationwide, business owners and collectors believe that non-mandated means non-regulated. Nothing could be further from the truth. Non-mandated collections are regulated by the Federal Department of Health and Human Services (DHHS).[17]

While states can make their own regulations, they cannot contravene or "step on" the federal rules. The federal DHHS rules clearly suggest that collectors follow federal regulations as a guideline. Simply put, the proper procedure for collections is to check one's ID, to empty their pockets of adulterants, to wash hands before and after the collection, to use blue dye and to follow all the other common sense chain of custody procedures that are mandated under the federal regulations.[18] This lack of specificity in the law invites those looking for loopholes a thousand ways to find them. Over the years, I have had many collectors tell me that, while they followed the guidelines in federal collections, they did whatever was convenient or time-saving for non-mandated collections since they erroneously believed there were no regulations.

A very specific, and disturbing, example of this by federal and non-mandated collectors is the sealing of the specimen tubes. In a federal collection, the collector must put the seals on the tubes, date the seals after they have been affixed to the specimen tubes then have the donor initial to ensure that it is the donor's specimen. [19] Again and again, I learn of collectors who do not follow this in non-mandated collections or in federal collections. Collectors will tell me that it is awkward to have the donor initial the security strip on the tubes, so since it is not mandated they allow the donor to initial the strip while it is still on the chain of custody form, then the collector removes it and hopefully places it on the correct specimen tube. This flies in the face of the intent of this step which is to ensure that the specimen was that of the donor. I don't know about you, but if I were a donor, I would want to know that every step was being taken to ensure that my specimen is not mixed up with anyone else's. Yet, time and again I see, and hear of, collectors doing this very thing because it is "easier" and, of course, it's not mandated! Sadly at my seminars and consulting sessions, this is just one of the many things which I discuss that put countless numbers of non-federal employees at risk of receiving false positive drug test results.

As if this issue were not enough, there are still other loopholes in non-mandated drug testing. Non-federal employers use all the loopholes that the mandated employers use and feel confident in using many more. For instance, non-mandated employers will use temporary agencies for many reasons, including but not limited to unemployment issues, tax and disability issues, and to get around liability for drug testing issues.

What non-mandated employers don't realize is that under drug and alcohol testing, mandated or not, the employer is ultimately responsible for the actions of all of their service agents directly or indirectly involved in the drug and alcohol testing process.[20] For instance, job placement agencies are hired first and foremost to provide employees for vacant positions. It's common practice for these agencies to either provide their own in-house testing or look for the cheapest collection providers available. Their priority is on placing people not the quality of the people they place or the integrity of the drug testing process. They completely disregard the conflict of interest in doing their own testing.

I have drug tested many former placement agency personnel and non-regulated HR personnel. The overwhelming majority of them have shared the frustration they felt in their former jobs where the unwritten policy on drug testing was to make sure people pass at any cost. It was made very clear to them that their job was to fill jobs not to worry about whether job applicants were drug free. While many anguished over the fact that they could either have their integrity or their job unfortunately, I have not met many who could afford to choose their principles over their paycheck.

My company has rarely been asked to provide testing services for job placement agencies. I firmly believe this is the result of its' reputation for integrity in the collection process. During a recent marketing campaign, my company offered significantly reduced prices to the employment/ temporary agency industry. RDTS did not have one taker and I, for one, was not surprised. It is, and has always been, the practice of my company to qualify its' clients not the other way around. Interestingly, while it received no response on a regional level, it actually does provide services to many of these companies on the national level.

FIRST: The instant screen

One of the biggest loopholes is the instant screen. The three-minute screen between the collector and the job applicant opens the door to discrimination, desperation and intimidation. It's the collector's personal call to decide how to read the result on that particular day.

An instant screen is a series of litmus strips similar to a pregnancy test. Each strip has a chemical identifier for a particular drug, marijuana, cocaine, opiates, amphetamines, etc. When the urine touches the strip, an identifier in the strip will be activated *only* if the matching identifier in the donor's system contains that particular drug. An instant screen is usually read by identifying the lines that appear on each litmus strip. It must be read within the specific time frame allotted by the manufacturer typically between two to five minutes. If it is read outside of the recommended time frame, the results are not valid. The first line usually will indicate that the test strip is working properly. A second line will appear if there is an absence of the target drug in the specimen. All the screens that I am aware of create a red line as an indicator. All the screens explain that a line is a line no matter how light or dark that line may appear. The absolute absence of the second line indicates that the drug targeted on that particular strip is positive. Marijuana and cocaine are seldom confused with other identifiers in the human body. However, opiates, amphetamines and other drugs may appear with the use of certain prescription drugs or illegal drugs. Instant screens have variable cutoff tolerances. They are highly sensitive to expiration dates and storage conditions. An instant screen indicates "yes" or "no" that a drug is in your system. It is not capable of determining if that particular opiate or amphetamine originates from a prescription, over the counter, or illegal drug.

The biggest issue that comes up in reading these results is the collector's personal insistence that the faintest line somehow indicates borderline drug use. This is absolutely false. A line is a line no matter how faint or dark that line is. Another issue that arises is the discussion between the donor and the collector about the presence of the line which ultimately affects the outcome of the test. This can range from discussing whether the lighting or the collector's eyesight is bad all the way to intimidation by the donor to the collector or vice versa. Why would the collector have any stake in whether there is a line? Well, consider who the collector may be. For example, if the collector is a parole or probation officer who thinks that the parolee or probationer in front of him should return to jail, the line may not show up. How about the employer who cannot afford to fire a longtime employee or relative especially when short staffed? Finally, consider the timid, non-confrontational collector who is going to see anything the overbearing, intimidating donor tells him or her to see. I think you get the picture. By the way, these are not hypothetical situations or just "hype" for this book. These are actual situations that I continue to see repeated every day. The results of the instant screen are often directly aligned with the agenda of the collector or the employer.

The litmus strips are also easily manipulated by the donor. While there are dozens of ways any donor with access to the Internet can fake an instant screen, I will only share one in this book. My intent is not to create a "how to" for drug users. If a drug user simply drinks an excessive amount of water, the litmus strip will indicate the test strip is working. It will also indicate no drugs have been detected in the donor's system. The reason for this controlled negative result is the litmus strip is testing excess water/fluid in the donor's system. (see Dilute Specimen in Glossary).

In the majority of our fifty states, instant screens are legal. However, they are the most widely misused product in the industry. The company I work for is based in New York State. Our home state prohibits the use of instant screens for any employment purpose. [21] I have been on a first-name basis with the head of New York State's DHHS collection compliance for many years. This is a subject that has frustrated and angered me from the day I started the business until present. New York State Public Health law Article 5 Title 5 requires the following:

> No person shall own or operate a clinical laboratory located in or accepting specimens from New York State or own or operate a blood bank which collects, processes, stores and/or distributes, human blood, blood derivatives or blood components, in New York State unless a valid permit has been issued as provided in section five hundred seventy-five of this title.

> "Clinical laboratory" means a facility for the microbiological, immunological, chemical, hematological, biophysical, cytological, pathological, genetic, or other examination of

materials derived from the human body, for the purpose of obtaining information for the diagnosis, prevention, or treatment of disease or the assessment of a health condition or for identification purposes

In my communications with the DHHS, I was advised that this applies to all workplace testing.

Even though this is New York law, the state refuses to address the issue that these prohibited screens are widely used and sold throughout the state. The loophole for the collector is this: It is not illegal to buy or sell these products it is only illegal to use them in an employment setting and to read the results. State and government agencies are commonly believed to be exempt from these restrictions. Laboratories and manufacturers of these products target and sell them, in bulk to employers throughout the state with full knowledge of their intent to be used in employment situations. This is not only a violation of law but an affront to an employee's right to compliant drug testing. Interestingly, all manufacturers of the instant screen recommend laboratory confirmation of the initial screen even in the states where they are legally allowed.

(*I have asked NYS DHHS for this citation several times over the years and once again for the express purpose of this book. At the time of writing this book, NYS -DHHS has not provided the law or regulation that allegedly allows this exemption to county, state and government agencies i.e.; courts, probation, rehabilitation etc.)

One incident that continues to frustrate me for more than ten years is a statewide provider of home and office cleaning services. In a face-to-face discussion with the hiring agent for this company, it was revealed that instant tests were used in interviews. The interviews were conducted at restaurants, truck stops and the like throughout the state for the purpose of "pre-qualification" better known as discrimination. This person looked me in the eye and said, "If they fail the test but they are clean-cut and I like them I will hire them." If they pass the test and don't look right or I don't like them I will find a problem with reading the results giving me a reason not to hire them." Each time I test a former employee of this company, or an applicant who was discriminated against by their drug testing "program", I am reminded of that conversation. I have consistently reported this to

45

the authorities who oversee drug testing compliance. I can tell you, with more than a little frustration, nothing has been done and this practice continues. And did I mention I also call that very person I had the conversation with? I inform her each time I see yet another dissatisfied former employee or applicant. I tell her I reported her to the authorities and I recommended that the employee/applicant do the same. Her response? Laughter! And why not? The authorities have done NOTHING to stop this in any way. She has no fear of any consequence for this clear, repeated violation of the drug testing laws.

SECOND: Pre-notification

Another loophole that non-mandated companies use is pre-notification of drug testing. These companies will suggest that the job applicant buy a home drug test before completing the application process. Another method of pre-notification is to give the job applicant anywhere from several days to several weeks to complete the drug test before the actual hire date. This allows the donor time to clean his system just long enough to pass the pre-employment test. Many companies eliminate random drug testing altogether. Any applicant that can stay clean long enough to pass the pre-employment test knows that once he has the job, there are no checks and balances to keep him drug free.

Many companies will also outsource sub-contractors who are not required to do drug testing. You may be surprised to learn that many companies who do not drug test are in-home service providers, such as housekeepers, day care, elder care, home health aides, plumbers and electricians just to mention a few. They are, however, very clever in leading you to believe that they are drug free by emphasizing that the company is bonded, insured, and conducts background checks.

Given the vulnerability of the people receiving these services, I was interested to know how many of these types of companies actually drug test. Posing as a potential client, I contacted many of these types of companies in a variety of geographic locations. In the initial contact, almost every one of them claimed to drug test their employees. When pressed further on the issue, the common response was that they drug test "at their discretion." Pressing a little further often resulted in being told that they hire people who they know or who are recommended to them. In other words, they don't drug test. These are the people most likely, if on drugs, to leave the back door open or make a copy of the key to your home to secure another source of revenue for their drug habit. I recall a situation where an exterminator entered a home and found drug paraphernalia in the bedroom of the homeowner's teenage son. The exterminator, who was a drug user, felt quite confident in taking what he wanted since any claim against him could easily be passed off on the son.

I do not offer this as an indictment of the entire "in home" industry. I am sure there are many trustworthy companies providing these services. But after what I have personally witnessed, I feel responsible to expose what I have seen. I also offer solutions to the consumer when faced with choosing a provider of any of these services. Thoroughly check out who you are allowing into your home. How can this be done? Ask about the drug testing policy. Ask who the collector/collection facility is. Ask if they do random testing and if they can provide you with verification of a random test program. This does not violate any privacy laws since you are not asking to see any specific test results. You are asking only to see the particulars of the overall drug testing program that is in place.

Oh, yes, don't forget to verify that they are actually doing the testing. While that may sound a little extreme, let me share a recent experience that I had. My company was asked to provide a quote for offering a drug testing program to one such service provider. I happily worked up the quote for a complete program which typically includes pre-employment, random, post accident and reasonable suspicion testing. A couple of weeks later, I received several phone calls complimenting me on landing a rather large client of home and commercial cleaning services. I was a little puzzled to say the least as I had never heard back from the company after giving them the quote. Upon further investigation, I discovered that they were telling their clients that they had a drug testing program and that my company was the provider! While one brief phone call to the company ended that quickly it did not help the customers who were duped into thinking they had drug- free employees working in their homes and businesses. Remember, you are talking about people who are caring for your children, working in your homes or businesses, caring for elderly loved ones and the list goes on. You have the ability, and more importantly the right, to know who is in your home. Any business that wants you as a customer should be more than happy to answer your questions about this critical issue.

Companies rely heavily on background checks as a substitute for drug testing. Background checks are extremely inexpensive and to the lay person, very impressive. Now, I am not talking about the background checks conducted for top security clearance at the CIA. I am talking about your average corporate/employment level background check. While it is certainly valuable for a day care center to know if a potential employee has been convicted of child molestation, or for a financial institution to know if a person has been convicted of embezzlement or larceny, this is past history. Background checks only tell you who has been caught and served their time. It does not tell you who has been arrested, who is awaiting trial, or who may have drug or alcohol issues. The background check gives a false sense of confidence for a fraction of the cost of drug testing. Drug testing will tell you that the potential employee is doing something right now. If someone is abusing drugs it is likely that they are stealing to support their habit.

I have drug tested many professionals in state and federal rehabilitation programs over the years who just can't seem to get kicked out of the program no matter how many times they fail a drug test, violate protocol or repeatedly change job locations within the same industry. Many professional substance abuse rehabilitation programs are conceptually sound but fall short of proper implementation, commonsense and enforcement.

It is also common to allow suspected child/sex offenders, embezzlers and drug users to leave their current job rather than be fired or arrested in order to protect a company or the institutions public image. We all know about national incidents which reveal decades of cover-up. I hear about, and personally know of, teachers, money managers, day care workers and medical professionals who mysteriously move from job to job with whispers of such allegations on a regular basis.

There are dozens of other loopholes commonly used by businesses that are not mandated to do drug testing that I address in my seminars, trainings and consulting.

4. Collector Loopholes

The collector is ultimately responsible for the integrity of the chain of custody. From the introduction of the donor to be tested straight through to the packaging of the specimens and the pickup by the designated courier to the lab, the collector is the common denominator. Prior to August 1, 2001, thousands of entrepreneurs and medical facilities performed drug testing with no uniform regulations or oversight. After 2001, collectors were required to become certified in compliance with the Department of Transportation and all of its modes. (FMCSA, FAA, FRA, USCG, etc.[22] However, no provisions were made for certification approval. This opened the door for another industry of unregulated providers called certification providers. Soon, meeting rooms across the country were flooded with active collectors desperate to meet the new certification deadline. In reality, these were nothing more than mass certification producers with misleading credentials.

In my search to obtain the required certification, I found the most recognized of a handful claiming to be "DOT approved" certification trainers. My training dates revolved around a trade show in Rhode Island and consisted of a one-day drug certification training. The class contained approximately seventy to eighty people who were already in business looking to get certified. The trainer had no practical experience as a collector and consistently misquoted the Code of Federal Regulations (CFR').

Another problem was attendees being allowed to complete both certifications in one day. The program offered drug certification and alcohol certification over two days. The intent appeared to be for an attendee to complete drug training one day and alcohol training the next. I observed participants jumping between the two classes on the same day and spending much time in the hallways conversing with other attendees or on cell phones. At the end of the day, these attendees walked out with two certifications when, in reality, the time they actually spent could not possibly have qualified them for one. They were allowed to get the same certifications as those of us who had spent the entire day in one session. As if this were not enough, the attendees were not made to perform the mock collections as required by the CFR'.

To add insult to injury, I was given the opportunity to have the business "accredited". The only requirement for this accreditation was an additional fee of fifty dollars.

Upon my return, I called this nationally recognized mass certification provider and voiced my complaints and concerns. I was advised that while their trainer was less than well versed in the CFR training, they had a three-year contract with the trainer which had to be honored. The next call made was to the DOT who advised me there was, in fact, no such approval. In fact, DOT said that they did not approve, certify, or endorse certification providers. The best they offered was a review of a proposed training course outline with recommendations if they saw fit. Then, and today, anyone who devises a course outline reciting CFR 49 Part 40.33 can claim to be approved or meet the standards/ requirements as a DOT certification provider.

Dissatisfied with the results, and frustrated with my inability to find competent collectors, I was determined to design a certification program that would meet all the requirements of the CFR' while producing properly trained collectors. My first thought was to train in small groups only, no mass certifications here. While this is not the cash cow approach it allows the trainer to assess the best way to present to each attendee. In addition, no cell phones or other distractions are allowed and the time actually spent training is strictly enforced. Finally, the required mock collections which is a requirement often skipped by most trainers are completed in strict accordance with the DOT regulations.[23]

Next, my thoughts went to the training materials. Realizing that proficiency is not achieved in an eight-hour training course, I was determined to develop materials that collectors could use in the field. The result was the *Rapid Drug Test Systems* training manual which doubles as a quick reference field guide for collectors. With feedback from hundreds of collectors in the field, the manual has been perfected to its current state. Many collectors whom I have trained tell me that they carry and use the guide in their daily work as do I.

During the course of one of my early trainings, a collector said "I wish I had you with me when a union rep tried to intervene during the middle of a collection." While we discussed this specific scenario, it was clearly too late to do anything about it. However, this made me think. Why can't I be there? Since that early date, I have offered one year of ongoing phone support to any trainee. I believe that my company is the only one that offers such a service. Many collectors have come back and told me that this was invaluable especially when faced with unusual situations which require split-second judgment calls. In addition to helping the collector get to the right answer, I find that this builds great confidence in the collectors in the field.

Shortly after my experience with the drug testing certification, I had a similar ordeal with alcohol certification. The provider of our breath alcohol device scheduled a training at my home for myself and eight collectors for an agreed one hundred and seventy five-dollars per attendee. When the trainer arrived, she immediately expressed her need to return to her home and offered to certify all of the attendees for thirty-five dollars each if she could give us the "abbreviated" version of the training. What was supposed to be a full day of training turned out to be a few hours, but she gave us the manuals and all the equipment needed to give us the basic gist of collecting samples. Unlike our experience with the drug certification company, the company this woman worked for was mortified, dismissed the trainer and offered me a three-day "train the trainer" course given by their senior trainer. Since then, I have had a ten-year relationship with this company in which they have referred trainings to me in my geographic area.

I have spent quite a lot of time here relating my experience with training and my continued disappointment with the industry, as these practices still continue to this day. Despite the attempts to undermine drug testing programs by employers, the collector remains the key to the integrity of the drug test collection. When a donor claims that his test results are not accurate, or there is a wrongful termination dispute, it is always the collector and the collection process that is attacked first. The quality and the integrity of the collector are paramount to the entire process.

Sadly, not all collectors are created equal. Even the best training programs will not deter the collectors who are determined to find loopholes, are ill-equipped and often times improperly trained or just plain lazy.

Whether collectors are federally mandated or are conducting collections under forensic non-mandated rules set by the DHHS, the protocol always puts the responsibility for the entire collection process on the collector. [24] For instance, the collector must personally verify the donor's identification. This cannot be done by a receptionist in another room.

FIRST: Specimen temperature

The collector must be prepared to complete all collections, including those which require opposite sex observation. Opposite sex backup is required when the temperature of the specimen is out of range. For example, the most common loophole of collector's is simply ignoring the temperature of a specimen instead of using opposite sex back up. It also occurs when the donor displays products or items that may be used to adulterate their specimens or for return to duty and follow-up testing, which is required for post-rehabilitation conditions. In these instances, the collector would ignore the temperature or use this loophole for many reasons. The temperature, which should be between ninety and one hundred degrees, may be out of range because the donor brought in someone else's urine. The specimen may also be much higher than the acceptable one hundred degrees because the donor brought in someone else's urine and then heated it with a device purchased on the Internet. Many of these devices bring the specimen temperature to one hundred and twenty degrees or higher. This requires the collector to package the original specimen and then conduct a second collection under observed collection protocol. This must be done by a same sex collector and is extremely invasive. The donor must pull his/her pants/skirt and underpants to the knee and lift their dress or shirt to the ribs and turn around three hundred and sixty degrees to show the collector that no strap on or foreign device is being used. The collector must then actually observe the urine pass from the donors body into the collection container. It is much easier, and far less confrontational, to just ignore the temperature. Other reasons may be due to donor intimidation or employer request to bypass this requirement. I have been asked by employers to do this many times. I have also had donors offer me cars, cash and sex or even the threat of being accused of sexual misconduct for not ignoring the temperature. Donors who are required to perform observed collections almost always insist no other collector does it properly. In my extensive search for subcontractors, I rarely find experienced collectors who follow protocol or even know what it is.

SECOND: Signing prior to obtaining specimen

This loophole was mentioned previously under forensic/ non-mandated loopholes and is worth mentioning again because it is so prevalent in both DOT and Non DOT collections. The collector instructs the donor to sign the chain of custody and initial the specimen bottle labels prior to the actual order in the process. This gives the donor an absolute defense against any positive due to the irregularity in the chain of custody. This will always result in the dismissal of the test result because you have no clear way of knowing that the specimen is, in fact, that of the actual donor. This is an all-too frequent occurrence that causes the results to become invalid in many disputed positive tests. These are just two of the many loopholes and tricks of the trade discussed in-depth during my consultations and training courses.

Since the employer is responsible for its collectors and service agents, it only makes sense that they familiarize themselves with the process they are relying on. But, how do they do that? How does the business owner know what to ask or what to look for in a collector or collection facility? Choosing quality collectors is really quite simple. Once the employer receives a copy of the collector's certification, they should verify its authenticity (Oh, did I mention that the business owner should *always* demand a copy of the certification?) Let me explain. Contact the provider of the certification and verify that the certification provider is real.

I learned that a collector was representing that he was certified by my company when, in fact, he was not. This collector had gone to an office supply store, purchased blank certificates, printed his name with my company logo and presented them as proof of his certification! Fortunately, the employer was on the ball and checked the credentials. The impersonator was immediately advised to cease and desist. After confirming that the certification provider is legitimate, the next, and most crucial question, is to ask if mock collections were performed at the time of the training. I am not aware of any online training programs that effectively address the mandatory mock collections required in the certification process.

The employer can ask the prospective collector for a copy of the collection procedures that they can expect to be implemented by the collector. This can also be found on the back of the donors' copy of the chain of custody form or DOT website. [25]

Many employers are unaware that it is mandatory for the designated employee handling the drug testing program, i.e. safety manager, HR, profit and loss supervisor, to complete a supervisor, substance abuse awareness training. [26] This qualifies them not only to properly recommend an employee for a reasonable suspicion test, but also familiarizes them with their responsibilities and the collection process.

5. REHABILITATION LOOPHOLES:

So why am I talking about rehabilitation in this book especially since I am neither a mental health professional nor a traditionally trained or certified counselor? I have never worked for a traditional drug and alcohol rehabilitation facility or organization. Allow me to explain why I believe my approach is more realistic for overall success over traditional methods.

We have all heard the saying. "If it were easy everyone would be doing it." Well, there you go. There are tens of thousands of rehabilitation programs that focus primarily on the addict. There is an extremely low expectation of success. In my experience over the past thirty years, those who complete a thirty day, six month or one year program generally come out "clean and sober." It is extremely rare that anyone stays that way for a full year. Most are back in addiction within a short time, if not immediately upon release, and experience multiple attempts at recovery. It mirrors the recidivism rates for people in jail. Rehab centers, as a rule, focus on the addict and spend minimal time working with the families and enablers of the addict. While many rehab centers have different programs, generally every program is pre-determined to end on a certain date. Addicts will tell you that they are in the "thirty day" or the "six month" or the "ten day intensive in-patient" program. The bottom line is that the program ends whether you are ready or not.

Rehabilitation is not cheap. These centers are well paid for their programs usually by insurance. I get families referred to me for consulting after their child or loved one has been through three, four or five traditional rehabilitation programs. The insurance is not willing to pay again. The nonprofit agencies have been exhausted and in many cases the savings/retirement are gone, the house is mortgaged or the family is on the edge of bankruptcy. These families are on the verge of giving up and view me as their last resort.

Every story is basically the same. The first program is usually local and takes a young, basically naïve experimenter and turns them into a more educated and savvy manipulator after being exposed to a group of far more experienced addicts. No one has prepared the family, friends and other enablers for the new and "improved" addict. While well intended, ex-addicts sitting around sharing their war stories turns out to be nothing less than a university-quality education for the beginner who learns new, improved ways to go home and manipulate family and friends who are expected to provide the aftercare. I cannot help but recall the "former" addict whose family told everyone that his time away was spent "at college" when in fact he was in rehab. This is not a mindset that is going to help anyone stay clean. Sadly, it did not help him.

So with the expectation of a high recidivism rate and a ready supply of insurance money where is the accountability for success? In my opinion the vast majority of the single digit percentage that can claim being cured often had the potential and the support to be successful eventually. They were going to be cured without rehabilitation anyway. Almost every recovered addict I speak to wishes the families knew about my approach while they were in rehab. It is unanimously agreed that educating enablers is key to recovery. There are only two reasons it is not being done by everyone. First, it is not easy and second, it is not profitable for the rehabilitation provider. The fact that it works is not relevant to the bean counters and the bottom line.

Second, third, fourth and fifth rehabs usually succeed in convincing the user that nobody cares about them. The user has heard it all over and over again. The approach is very much "one size fits all." The user keeps going through the program which is the same over and over again. The user quickly learns the "right" things to say to be declared "clean" only to be released from the program and use again. Some users will actually volunteer for short-term detoxification programs for the purpose of ensuring the next high has the quality of the first one that got them hooked. Yes, even the worst of addicts realize they have to reach a point when they are numb and only a self-imposed cleansing will allow them to achieve the high they so desperately crave.

I recall two unforgettable examples of this in action. The first involves a young lady in her twenties who had been using for ten years. The family comes in to complain about the numerous failed rehabs and the fact that the addict simply "does not get it." They have labeled her hopeless and loudly proclaim that they are at their wits end. At the end of the first meeting, every family member literally hates me because I have revealed that the addict would love to be cured but the family is incapable of recognizing and correcting their enabling behavior. They feel that I am attacking them and I am, because denial does not choose its accomplices. While I never say it aloud I often think if I were in the addict's shoes I, too, might consider resorting to an artificial source of relief maybe even drugs. In this particular case, the addict and I worked together to rebuild the addict's self-esteem by calling out and educating the enablers into realizing what had been at the core of the addicts drug use from the very beginning. For this addict, drug use was her response to and simply an excuse for her inability to communicate with family and friends she felt bound to. Unfortunately her continued success will depend on not allowing their continuing faults to be an excuse for her relapse.

The second, and most common, scenario that I face is families with pre-teen or teenage users. They are usually desperate to "fix" the child. At the conclusion of the first meeting, I often say out loud I don't recall offering myself as a surrogate parent. These are the hardest enablers to reach. The child is usually in full control of all the adults. With pre-teens and teens, the answer really lies in establishing authority. Once I convince parents that their job is simply to prepare their children to carry on successfully once they die, we start to make progress. The turning point seems to come when the parents realize that if they died in a car accident tomorrow there is no one to care for little Johnny. The typical conversation goes something like this: "When he comes home drunk from his friends, I can't just turn him away." They are usually shocked when I suggest that they take him back to the friend's house, let him throw up there and let him return only when he is sober. Or better yet, call the police and have the friends parents charged with contributing to the delinquency of a minor. This suggestion is often met with shocked looks and protests of "we don't want to cause trouble." What message is this sending to the child? I ask the parents, do you care more about offending the friend's parents or about your child? Getting their ex-spouses and second spouses, grandparents and immediate family to form a cohesive team is a huge battle. We quickly realize that the adults are incapable of putting the child's needs before their own. When the new spouse is blaming the former spouse or when the parent is at odds with the grandparent, the child is often lost in the adult agendas.

While this all sounds very discouraging, and often times is, there are bright spots and success stories. Here are a few testimonials from some parents and former users:

Testimonials

After several years of escalating drug use, failed rehabilitation, counseling and violent behavior with my single mom, I am on my way to recovery. After our first session your brutal but passionate no-nonsense approach put my mom and I on the same side for the first time in years. You offended us equally. In our quest to get even with you, we actually realized it was possible to communicate. At the end of our second encounter with you we realized you had a unique ability to evaluate and manipulate our ignorance into positive, eye-opening ways to work through our problems and my addiction. Once you made us realize my addiction was our problem, the healing began. Even though our third visit with you was our last we refer to your passion and fearless in-your-face logic that allows us to stay on point and continue to move forward. I will be starting college soon, and Mom and I will no doubt be referring to the brief but life-changing encounter we experienced with you. There are no words.

TD and Mom

My son had been using drugs since he was twelve years-old. We brought him to see you as a last resort at seventeen years-old and what looked like a certain future as a lost adult.

He had been kicked out of his forth rehab center and I had spent my life savings on psychiatrists, psychologists and drug counselors. None had insisted on involving the entire family. When you told my ex-wife and I to get our significant others, in-laws, future in-laws, siblings and future step-siblings to commit to being part of the solution I thought you were out of your mind. When I offered you money to compromise on that request, you told me to save the money for my son's funeral or career prison life and wished me luck and a good day. I knew at that moment you meant business. In short, my son is doing very well for a little over a year now. You showed us the light at the end of the tunnel in just a couple of weeks when years and tens of thousands of dollars brought us consistently further from hope with each day and dollar invested. You helped us create an internal support team that just simply cannot fail. Your influence has impacted so many more lives than just our immediate family. I now understand your comments as you ended our first interview. "There are too many people for me to help. If you don't get it by the third visit, you won't. Unfortunately for society, I don't need you to fail in order for me to survive. I have other families to schedule so do you want to try it my way or can I make time for someone who will?

Thank you for your straight-forward approach and sharing your many years of knowledge.

S.M., MD

My husband and I suspected our fifteen-year-old for months. You spoke to me several times and never asked our names or mentioned money. We finally convinced him to get tested and we are on the road to recovery."

Concerned mother of high school student

When I called I was concerned about the way my thirteen-year-old daughter was dressing, her new friends and attitude. After talking to you for a short time you made me realize there may be more to think about. Just minutes into our first visit you convinced her to be tested. She was positive for heroin. I was devastated and she was mad and in denial. Before we left you made sure we were communicating and assured both of us this was not the end of the world. The literature, advice, referrals and support have truly been a saving grace.

Single working mother

This should be a mandatory course for anyone who is a parent. So informational. Need more of these courses, especially in the schools!

…Very honest information that all parents and schools should be aware about. Comments from two sets of parents

Attendees at Broome Community
College Course
RDTS FYI ~ Family and Youth Initiative
"What Parents Don't Know
About Tweens and Teens"

Funding Drug Use

So often I am asked how the user can afford to do drugs. Users are very creative when they are desperate. I remember a grandmother wondering aloud how her grandson could possibly afford drugs. Upon being pressed a little further, she told me that she gave him ten dollars every day to go to the local fast food restaurant for his favorite meal. I asked her if she went with him. Of course she did not. Imagine her shock when she was made to realize that she was supporting her grandson's drug problem. This was an obvious one. Consider the father who was having trouble with the amount of gas his young son was using to drive around town. This kid needed "gas money" every other day! Then there's the mother who could not figure out why her postage stamps were disappearing from her desk. Every time she went to pay a bill or mail a letter, she did not have any stamps. I remember the parent's frustration with her daughter's inability to keep her cell phone for more than one week or consistently losing her iPod.

I made several suggestions to these people. Most of them shocked the parents and angered the user. Here they are - what do you think?

- If your grandson asks for money for food- either feed him at home or take him to the restaurant. You will find out- real fast- just how hungry he really is.

- Check the odometer when he takes the car, or better yet, take him to the gas station - no cash. And forget "gas cards." They can be sold for cash.

- Stamps are currently forty four dollars per roll. Selling at even half price brings enough cash to get high.

- Unless the teen is suffering from early onset Alzheimer's, she is most certainly selling all items of value for cash. (This one prompted some additional advice.) Lock the medicine cabinets, protect the credit cards, don't keep a lot of cash in the house and for goodness sake, don't keep buying her phones and iPods!

Then there is the thought that no parent wants to face. A mother and her fourteen year-old daughter came into my office. The young girl was barely dressed, her skirt revealed the color of her underwear and her shirt left little to the imagination. Her mother insisted that her daughter had no access to money or valuables with which to buy drugs. I responded to the mother by saying if I was a young man with drugs, I would give her whatever she wanted just to get the rest of what little she is wearing off of her. She does not need money. Sex is the new commodity. The mother was appalled at the suggestion and the daughter vehemently denied having sex, but quickly followed that up by saying that she did perform acts which she did not consider sex. Well, if it worked for the former president, why not for her?

Increasing Success

The bottom line is that there are just as few families interested in really helping the addict as there are rehabilitation facilities interested in helping the addict unless it is profitable. Until the two approaches come together, success rates will remain in the single digits. The above testimonials are the result of addicts and enablers growing together and remaining committed to the cause for however long it takes. These people stayed committed to the addict when it was not convenient to do so, when it did not fit their schedule, without regard to whether the money was running out. In short, they learned and expressed tough love and zero tolerance.

While tough love and zero tolerance sound great, both are extremely rare. Substance abusers are called users because they are just that. They use drugs, alcohol, friends, family, jobs and strangers. If your friend actively uses and says he/she understands and respects you for not using and continues to be your friend, you are not a true friend. You are being used for a ride to a place to use or meet others who use, the first drink that will end up being too many, an alibi or argument why he/she couldn't be using. A user doesn't respect people who don't approve of what they do. Users tolerate people who criticize what they do. You are simply an enabler. Tough love is not tough if it is convenient, inconsistent, used only in extreme situations or when the mood is right. Zero tolerance? Well what part of "zero" don't true friends understand?

When you decide to defend a user, without seeking to hear any other version or you utter any of the following: "I trust you," "well. just be careful," "just one," "just a little," "let me think about it," "don't worry I won't tell this time," "well what if," "Ok, just don't do it in front of me," you have enabled, condoned, approved, and encouraged the behavior. Being a true friend is like being pregnant or dead. Either you are or you are not.

We all have casual acquaintances and friends. Being a true friend is a commitment and a responsibility. Not everybody can be a true friend. It just isn't popular. It certainly isn't easy. True friends have a great deal of responsibility. A true friend will seek help to understand the problem. This is no time for on-the-job training. Parents and friends just don't seem to get it. If you are not in the industry, personally in touch with current issues or completely rehabilitated as a former problem user, you are not qualified to help. You might even make it worse. Users rarely feel understood.

You must find a licensed professional or industry expert that you trust. Getting advice is worthless if you don't trust and use it. Do not ask if you plan to tweak. Either you know what to do or you don't. We are dealing with human lives, not objects that can be re-glued or erased and tried again. Reading books certainly will help but nothing replaces first-hand knowledge and experience.

Substance abuse is only a symptom of a greater issue. Users need little reason to use again. Just by saying the wrong thing, you can easily be the unwilling excuse. Believe me a user will *make* you say the wrong thing. Users are masters at manipulation, imposing guilt, and lying.

It is my hope that the message you take away from this section is this: there are solutions. They are not always profitable or easy. But your friends, family members or loved ones are worth it. Stay with it!

FAMILIES

The previous section of this book featured a few testimonials. The common denominator of these successful interactions was creating a team between the addict and the enablers. In most cases, the conditions that lead to addiction start at a young age. Low self-esteem and lack of self-respect are generally present in the early stages. Add poor, or non-existent, communication between parent and child and you have the fertile ground which nourishes a full blown addict.

While I don't want to make a blanket statement that all addiction starts with bad parent's, I will say that many parents unintentionally love their children right into addiction and sometimes all the way to death. Early in my consulting with families, I usually start out comparing a parent's responsibilities for their children to that of parents in the animal kingdom.

It seems that human parent's are under so much social and political pressure that our basic instincts and duties take a back seat. In nature, an eagle, through instinct alone, feeds, nurtures and teaches its young what is necessary to survive on its own. When the time comes to throw the young one out of the nest, it is often from heights of thousands of feet. Has that parent taught that child first, how to fly, second how to feed himself and third how not to become someone else's meal? The goal of every wildlife family is to make sure that when the instinctive time comes for the young to become independent of their parents, the child has the ability to survive.

The Proper Support

In the human world, parents, grandparents, extended family and friends usually have to realize that the addict was not properly prepared for adulthood and would not be able to survive for long if they all disappeared tomorrow morning. While we all need support, the key is whether or not we have the proper support. We can't help others if we can't help ourselves. I find that in the end the key to success is when the addict finds his or her self-esteem and the enablers find theirs. After all, misery really does love company.

Our youth start their journey to drug, alcohol and other addictive behaviors years before they actually start "actively addicting" that is, using the substance that will become their drug of choice. Being raised by a single parent, the trauma of divorce, death, lack of finances and other obstacles are all convenient excuses for why we want to find alternative support. I find that once I get all the enablers together it is the addict who is usually most sincere and most committed to getting better and it is the addict who is willing to change in order to get there. I see the addict's self-esteem emerging once the enablers are exposed for their intentional or unintentional ability to be the proper sources of support.

This brings to mind the call I received from the friend of a distraught mother who asked me to call the friend. My first thought was if she can't make the initial phone call she is going to be the typical "drag them in, drag them around" enabler. I did place the call to this woman. She asked what I could do to help her daughter, who was in her mid-twenties and had been abusing pills since her early teens. I explained that I wanted to meet her, her significant other, the young lady's father, his significant other and anybody else who was in this young lady's life. I made it clear that I wanted to meet all of them *before* I met the daughter. After telling me every excuse she could find work schedules, babysitters, other people's schedules, etc., she did succeed in agreeing with me on a date and time.

At the first meeting (and, sadly, not to my surprise) only the addict showed up. She was completely wasted on pain pills. She impressed upon me how desperately she wanted help. She proceeded to recite a long list of emergency room visits, detox facilities, countless short-term and long-term rehabilitation facilities, and encounters with psychologists and psychiatrists that she had seen over the years. In short, she described a life of living hell. This first meeting ended with her asking me for a recommendation to a methadone or alternative drug treatment clinic. I told her that I was not a supporter of alternative drug treatment clinics. I also told her that she should not attempt to detox without medical supervision and never to see me stoned. She then asked if she would be allowed to come back even though she may only have one solid supporter. We scheduled a second meeting four days later.

She arrived for this meeting with her mother's boyfriend, a recovered addict himself with fifteen years of sobriety. She proudly announced that she had been clean since the last meeting four days of sobriety was a huge accomplishment for her. Over the course of the next few meetings, and with the help of the mother's boyfriend, we discussed and prepared her for the inevitable consequences of not using drugs that would most certainly begin to occur. While getting through this cleansing period, we also got to some of the core roots that drove her to choose drugs. These mostly revolved around her family and closest friends. In case you haven't noticed, the mother never attended one of these meetings nor did any other family member or friend. Several months passed and noticeable progress was being made.

This young lady was committed to breaking the confines of her surroundings. She was really grasping the concept of dealing with the people around her. I asked her why she kept coming back to me. She told me that I was the first person that did not talk down to her and listened to her as though she was an individual not just another "one size fits all" client. One of her dreams was to become a radio personality. Instead of giving her the standard "anything is possible" speech I took her to a local radio station. There, she was given a full tour, explanation of how things worked and an invitation to participate in a live radio interview that I had scheduled. For the first time, she actually could conceive that she would accomplish her goal. She felt so good that she convinced her mother to meet me.

During that first encounter with her mother, I realized immediately that there would be no hope for her if she did not get away from her mother. In short, the mother was the epitome of negativity, hopelessness and victim mentality. But it did not stop there. This woman had no ability to encourage anybody to rise above her own self-imposed prison of feeling worthless. I could see all hope drain from the young lady's face. As I suspected, I never saw either of them again. This is just one example of hundreds of people who have the same story. The names and faces may change, but the underlying elements repeat themselves over and over again.

Single Parents

Single parents frequently report working ten hour days to support their families. They will often spend hours telling me why they don't have time to spend with their child but don't realize that they can take that time while grocery shopping, doing laundry, and doing housework by simply including the child in that mandatory activity.

The following example is again one of hundreds. A mother of a seventeen year-old boy contacted me. She explained that her son had been using drugs since he was twelve and was completely out of control. I asked her to come, alone, to the first meeting. Predictably, she arrived at the meeting with her son. They had both said there was a lack of communication. Approximately ten minutes into this meeting, and after the fifth interruption from the son, I realized the son was in full control of that two person household. I abruptly declared my authority in my office. I shared my opinion about who the authority should be in that house. I informed the mother that I had no interest in seeing her, with her son, at our next meeting. I told the son exactly what would be tolerated if I were the parent.

Even though I clearly requested that the mother return alone, they came to the second meeting together. The meeting started with the mother defending her son and the son confirming how "they" wished to proceed with my consulting. They expressed how offended they both were by the first meeting. When they were finished, I replied that I could not help them if they did not tell me the truth. Remember, the biggest complaint was the lack of communication. They appeared to be communicating just fine, joined against a common enemy: me. You read the results of this meeting in a prior testimony which stated that I had offended them both equally. It seems that in these situations communication is not the problem, it is how they communicate that needs to be resolved.

Divorced Parents

Divorced parents usually seem to be divorced legally only. Many refuse to move on. They spend all of the child's rehabilitation time blaming each other and/or the ex's significant other. Countless hours are wasted rehashing all the issues the divorce should have settled. Even with their "new" lives and spouses, they still can't come together over the one and only mutual thing they cannot discard from their former union their addicted child. I had a grandmother contact me about her twenty three-year-old granddaughter who was living with her. She reported that her granddaughter had been using drugs since she was fifteen years-old. She felt that the divorce had led to the drug use. I agreed to meet with them. I further requested that the young lady's parents, both of whom were out of town, be available by phone. In speaking to the addicted young lady, it was revealed that the addiction began several years before the divorce. The entire family, including the grandmother, had their own bouts with gambling, drug and alcohol addictions. After five meetings, held over the course of several weeks, I had not heard from any family members other than the grandmother. She was not capable of completing a sentence without defending all the enablers in this young lady's life.

For several months, I agreed to work only with the young addict. When I eventually gathered all the family members together for a conversation, I highly recommended that they all seek professional help. I expressed complete understanding at how someone, who could not escape that environment, would turn to some alternative relief. The key to this young lady's success was to limit her exposure to these enablers without guilt of abandonment. Once she moved out of her grandmother's house, and limited her exposure to the barrage of negativity, she was able to appreciate her grandmother and other enablers in a different light.

Grandparents

It's especially hard dealing with grandparents who are far removed from the reality of this generation. It's hard to explain to a grandmother, a drug addict at any age, twelve, twenty two or forty two, is incapable of having genuine concern about the feelings of others. Over the years, I have had many concerned grandparents call with the frustration of not being able to trust their grandchildren in their homes.

I can't forget the grandparents who came to me about their sixteen year-old twin grandsons. The boys were high honor students, participated in sports, worked odd jobs and were popular. From outward appearances, these boys were "on the right track." These grandparents had heard from friends and relatives that they were involved in drugs and hanging with the wrong crowd. All attempts by the grandparents to discuss their concerns with the parents were rejected. After meeting the grandsons, I was able to impress upon the grandparents the need to addict proof their home and habits. If no one was going to help these kids with their addiction then these grandparents had to learn the measures to protect themselves and their property. This was a really hard concept for them to understand. They could not conceive why they would have to protect themselves and basically not trust the grandsons they loved so much. But without the support of the parents, these kids were not going to take any steps to get better. And they didn't. Eventually, drugs did what they always do. The boys dropped out of sports, their academics suffered and they both ended up with criminal records. The only thing the grandparents had was the peace of mind that they did not contribute to the decline of their grandsons. This was little comfort for two heartbroken grandparents. In my seminars, I have taught grandparents these very same steps measures that are designed to prevent theft from their homes and to eliminate the ongoing frustration caused by the addict.

The addict has to realize that he or she has to change the people, places and things or, at the very least, rise above them. If they cannot get physically away from their family members, they have to learn to recognize that family and friends have agendas, too. And they might have to learn to deal with them in spite of these faults.

COMMUNITIES

Communities can impact the effect of drug trafficking, drug dealers and drug addiction in the workplace, schools and in families. Earlier in this book, I mentioned that I grew up in the fifties and sixties. I recall knowing everyone in my neighborhood, and more importantly, everyone knew me. If you did something at your friend's house, your mother knew about it before you got home without the benefit of email, text messaging or Tweets. I am more than aware that our society has drastically changed. But if we want to solve the issues of drug traffic, gang activity and drug related crime, we better consider making yet another change.

That change starts with realizing that everyone needs to be involved to be part of the solution. We need to take responsibility for our communities. When you live across the street from a family with a drug addicted teen, it is easy to say, "Well, that's their problem." But is it really? Does it become your problem when he breaks into your house to steal and support his habit? Does it become your problem when his dealer "delivers" his product while your kids are playing outside? How does it affect you when he starts to grow and/or sell drugs from his home to support his habit? Guess what, it's not just "their" problem anymore.

Drug dealers and drug trafficking are like any other business. If there is a demand, they will fill it. If your community is experiencing a drug and gang problem, it is not because of any one sector of your community. Drug users, or the demand that invites drug traffic, drug dealers and drug- related crime to your community, starts in your schools, in your workplaces and with the residents in the community. In order for communities to conquer these issues, you have to understand how a community is sup- posed to function. This raises the following questions:

Who represents your community?

Are just public servants looked to for all the solutions?

No. Without you their agenda is politically driven. Public servants who are not involved with the community are not likely to address risky issues that can backfire and jeopardize their chances for re-election. The community that comes out only one day a year to vote for its leaders, and then sits back and expects the leaders to solve the problems for another two years, is not a community that can expect positive results in protecting their schools, workplaces and neighborhoods.

Does the community at large feel a sense of disconnect?

No. When a community feels disconnected from its public servants, a "them" vs. "us" mentality often takes root. This creates a distraction, taking the focus off the real issues. Drug dealers and addicts flourish in this environment. They take full advantage of the opportunity of being overlooked. While citizens and public servants focus all of their attention fighting *about* drugs and crime no one is actually fighting *against* drugs and the crime!

Is it a combination of the community and leaders working together?

Yes. This is the definition of community working together for the common good.

This requires that each part clearly understands their role. Community leaders and public servants need to do just that; serve the public. We seem to have lost that concept somewhere in the last few decades. At times it seems as though we work for our elected officials, not the other way around.

The members of the community have their role as well. They need to clearly, and consistently, let the leaders know their concerns and needs. Does your boss tell you what to do once every two or four years? I didn't think so. They need to stay with it. Consistency is key in this area. You can't start a Neighborhood Watch program for a couple of months and then stop. Like everything else in life, once you fix it, you have to maintain it.

The good of the community must come before personal and political agendas. Impossible, you say? Not really. You hire (elect) these people every two or four years. *You are not powerless.* The communities who find success are the ones that have active Neighborhood Watch programs which assist and guide their local law enforcement. They do not just simply show up for the meetings with a list of license plate numbers. Quite often these programs are started by the parents of drug users in hopes of scaring off those bad influences. The reality is the addict in the organizer's house becomes the source of information that enables the drug dealers and users to undermine the Neighborhood Watch program. You can prevent this by inquiring about the watch leaders, and children or even their spouses. Persistent rumors and sarcastic affirming comments from your children and other neighbors are usually a subtle warning of the truth. Do not enable this group by pretending the suspicions don't exist. Look for or start another group that doesn't protect those in denial. After each meeting, the addict tells everyone exactly what the police are up to and what they now know. In the world of drugs, things arc rarely what they seem to be.

When I think about this topic, a town supervisor from a small community comes to mind.

This highly energetic, committed public serv-
ant held emergency town meetings to address
specific issues like drug activity reported in iso-
lated neighborhoods. She created public forums
for her constituents who included local law
enforcement and other municipal leaders. But
she went one step further by inviting outside
independent consultants. The key to her success in ridding drug traffic for her constituents
was in implementing action that did not always
agree with political and law enforcement agendas. She understood that when it comes to drugs
and crime, time really is of the essence. It was
reported that her actions in eradicating drug
traffic had an immediate, far- reaching and
positive effect on her entire community. It was
also reported that her actions had a devastating
impact of law enforcement budgets, long-term
investigations and personal agenda's i.e. job pro-
motions. By eliminating the easy access for the
local drug users to obtain their desired drugs,
crime was reduced and home invasions ceased.
Including the community eliminated the apathy
that had been building from years of non-action
by law enforcement. It provided the members of
the community with a sense of pride and accomplishment a sense that they were not powerless.

That very special bond continues in her community to this very day and is helping them to meet the daily challenges created by the ever present threat of crime and drugs.

In the face of drugs, communities have to act like armies in a war. Citizens can no longer simply appoint the general or in this case mayors, supervisors or executives and disappear until the next election. The success story recited above was the perfect combination of a willing, capable leader and residents that got behind her and took action. The experience of that group can be repeated in neighborhoods, towns, and villages across the country if people are willing to get and stay involved. As with families, communities must also make diligence their goal. It is not enough to have one great accomplishment or clean out one neighborhood or create one neighborhood watch team. This is a war; the enemy is well equipped, patient and dedicated.

LAW ENFORCEMENT

EXPECTATIONS vs. REALITY

Law enforcement comes with certain expectations. The common expectation is that law enforcement professionals are above the law. We believe that they are there to serve and protect. The victim is their utmost priority.

Another expectation of enforcing the law is if you break the law you get arrested. The reality is law enforcement professionals often use a variety of factors to "decide" if the offender is going to be arrested. Some considerations are whether the offender is valuable to law enforcement. If the offender has some information or connection that is useful to law enforcement, especially in the context of a long-term investigation, (more on this later). there is usually a reason found not to arrest the criminal. Fear of retaliation is sometimes used as a way to deter the victim from bringing charges. I personally experienced this with law enforcement professionals who "suggested" that I not press charges in connection with property that had been stolen. I was cautioned that the offenders might return and do worse.

Oftentimes, the cost in time, paperwork and court appearances is weighed against the value of the outcome. Let me illustrate with a story. Several homeowners were robbed of household goods, the usual stuff computers, televisions, and cameras, items that are quickly turned into cash by the criminals. When this was reported, the homeowners were advised that pressing charges would require that they complete numerous police reports, talk to an assistant district attorney and/or the investigator and possibly testify at a trial that would eat up yet additional time. The ultimate question was then put to these homeowners: Do you really want to go through all of this or can't you just report it to your insurance and get all new stuff? Several homeowners were shocked at the cavalier attitude of these law enforcement professionals.

This practice does not only appear in situations where the criminal is let off the hook. I have listened to story after story of individuals who were involved in traffic accidents where both parties were given tickets even though one was clearly at fault. This also seems to be a common occurrence in domestic disputes.

Now, I am not questioning the judgment of law enforcement professionals in every situation. Exercising their judgment in sometimes the most difficult of situations is what we pay them for and what we want them to do. However, we need to know that judgment is going to be based on what laws have been broken and what is best for the victim not based on the agenda of the particular police department or the value of that particular criminal is to the police.

Long-term Investigations:

For decades, long-term drug investigations have been sold to the public as the only way to get to the "kingpin" the drug suppliers, the head of the snakc. In reality, long-term investigations guarantee the growth of the drug industry and the crime related to it.

This was proven to me over and over again during my three years of work with federal, state and county law enforcement agencies. In my role as a deep undercover operative, I oversaw more than one hundred million dollars of drug trafficking and sales in a relatively small geographic area. Multiply that by the entire United States! For those who may not be aware there is a difference between "undercover" and "deep undercover." Traditional undercover is when law enforcement officers go to work and conduct investigations as part of their job duties. Typically, when their vacation comes up or they have days off the investigations get put on hold or conducted between their other duties. "Deep" undercover is when law enforcement operatives, or informants, take on their undercover identity 24/7. It becomes your life, criminals become your family and you put your former identity aside if you want to survive. In my case, my family and friends believed that I had become a real organized crime drug dealer. I let them believe it for three long years. It was crucial to my success and survival. I didn't have the luxury of going home to my real life at the end of each day.

Fighting drugs with long-term investigations doesn't serve any benefit. Later in this book, you will have the opportunity to read an essay by Mike Levine that addresses this very issue. As one of the nation's most highly decorated former DEA agents, who served a thirty five year career as an international federal narcotics officer, trial consultant, expert witness, and bestselling author of books exposing the failed war on drugs, Mr. Levine's experiences and insights are truly eye opening. In order to conduct a long-term investigation, you must ensure that ongoing drug sales, drug crimes and drug trafficking survive and prosper for long periods of time.

To deter drug activity on any level would only serve to undermine a long-term investigation. While our local, county and state law enforcement agencies claim to be chasing the "kingpins," I can assure you the DEA and CIA are working closely with all of them for international political agendas.

Law enforcement is intended to be an extension of the citizens. Long term investigations have made the citizens acceptable collateral damage necessary to secure funding. Let me explain, from the beginning, how these investigations work. Generally, on the local level a few neighbors may call their local police department to report suspicious activity in a single home on their street. They may report traffic in the neighborhood of five cars per hour. A Neighborhood Watch officer will be assigned to the residents of that neighborhood to assist in forming a neighborhood watch program. This usually consists of the residents getting together once a week, twice a month or monthly to report license plates numbers and descriptions of the people frequenting the address of concern. Typically, after six or seven months of reporting the activity, which by now has grown from five or six cars an hour to ten to twenty cars an hour, the residents have grown anxious and begin to demand some action from the police as the problem appears to be getting worse. The residents are usually met with the following rationale: the people coming into your neighborhood are part of a much bigger picture, so the investigation must continue a little longer. When the residents finally realize that law enforcement agendas have only made their small situation worse, law enforcement will conduct a raid netting a handful of customers frequenting that address. This is clearly done to appease the residents. But the damage from the investigation is done. There is still a surplus of criminals operating at the same location. So where is the benefit to the long-term investigation?

Long-term investigations rarely serve as a deterrent to drug related crime and activities in communities. When I came out from undercover, I started consulting business owners, landlords and residents how to deter drug and crime activity and to undermine long-term investigations that ensured the growth of such activity. Years later, I became aware of Mike Levine, an internationally renowned, retired DEA agent who had written several bestselling books[27] on the failed war on drugs. Mike Levine and I came together over one book he had written that was geared towards citizens taking back their neighborhoods, schools and families from the drug dealers.[28] I am repeatedly called upon to talk about this topic and to consult neighborhoods in how to take back their neighborhoods safely, anonymously, quickly and inexpensively.

I cannot discuss this topic without recalling the story of what a group of concerned citizens faced when they insisted on finding solutions to the drug problems in their Ohio neighborhood. At the time, a grandmother from Warren, Ohio, contacted Mike Levine, who graciously referred her to me. She had been responsible for organizing more than a dozen Neighborhood Watch committees. She also worked with several police departments, mayors and an array of politicians. Her name was well-known to local television stations, talk show radio hosts and other media. Although her organization was growing, and working tirelessly to stem the problem, she was frustrated with the lack of results she was seeing. It was this frustration that caused her to be referred to me.

After just a few phone calls, at my recommendation, she arranged a conference call which consisted of politicians, law enforcement and numerous Neighborhood Watch organizers. The immediate agreement was that her organizations were going to hold fundraisers to bring me and Mike Levine, to a mass event in the Youngstown/ Warren communities. Within just a few days, her support from law enforcement, politicians and some media splintered as I had predicted. Almost immediately, Neighborhood Watch coordinators were divided and expected to choose between the established organizations or to bring in us, the outside consultants for quick results. After a few short weeks, she was once again starting over having been abandoned by those who enjoyed the "idea" of being part of Neighborhood Watch but did not want to participate in taking real action. After several months, she had organized a much smaller, but highly committed, group of citizens who were ready to take action. Her persistence and tenacity inspired me to go out and assist her.

To promote the event, in the eleventh hour, she had pulled together several radio talk show interviews, television interviews and had booked a lecture hall at Kent State University. During the media blitz, all politicians, law enforcement and media staunchly supported her. The night I arrived she had scheduled a ride along with the local police department and had raised enough money to cover my expenses. The police took me into the roughest, drug-infested neighborhoods in their community. When we arrived at Kent State for the forum, none of the public servants who had participated in the media blitz showed up. I found it curious that they all found time to grand stand for the radio and TV promos, which were heard by tens of thousands of constituents, but could not appear at the forum, where the audience was approximately one hundred and fifty. Eventually she was completely abandoned and her efforts dismantled. This scenario has been repeated in Tennessee and dozens of other communities nationwide.

As I have been called upon to assist citizens in many parts of the country, it has been my experience that these citizens who wish to take back their neighborhoods meet with resistance from law enforcement, media and politicians. The tactics that I teach to neighborhoods immediately threatens long-term investigations. These tactics have been studied by universities and institutes. They were endorsed by former President Clinton and supported by law enforcement agencies across the country, that is, until the potential for absolute success was realized. Now, residents using these tactics will be immediately met with opposition from law enforcement, media and politicians whose agendas, budgets and jobs are threatened by its success. The war on drugs has become a trillion- dollar business. Criminals and crime can survive just fine without politicians and law enforcement. However, law enforcement and politicians cannot survive without crime, especially crime generated by drugs, and the billions of dollars that this brings in the form of grants and program funds.

COMMUNITY RESPONSIBILITIES:

While the section above ends with what seems like a failure it should be viewed as a lesson for communities. Residents fail when they allow politicians and police to rule them. Many of the people in the previous examples succeeded on their streets and in their neighborhoods despite opposition from the public servants paid by their tax dollars to protect them. The community efforts that failed allowed their public officials to put their agendas ahead of those who pay them.

It is the community's responsibility to realize that voting day should be nothing more than picking the person who will take direction from the majority, not the majority placing everything in that person's hands to do as they will.

During the course of my consulting, I have spoken with numerous individuals who claim they want to be good citizens and "do the right thing," but then add that no one likes a snitch, rat or stool pigeon. I quickly try to negate this perception by asking about their definition of a snitch, rat or a stool pigeon. It is a criminal or other wrong-doer who is trying to save their own neck or divert attention to another wrong-doer/criminal. Citizens have an obligation to inform law enforcement of illegal and/or suspicious activity. They also have the pre-paid right paid for by their tax dollars to expect action and protection. This does not make the citizen a snitch, rat or stool pigeon. The citizen has no way to enforce the law. That would be vigilantism which is not being suggested here. The citizen supports law enforcement and law enforcement respects, and protects, the citizen.

As individuals, this is not always the way it works. In true communities where citizens and law enforcement work together it does work. When law enforcement is allowed to choose agendas over the needs of citizens, then communities have an obligation to take full advantage of their rights under the Constitution. These include the right to public protest, the right to attend and participate in public meetings and the right to freely speak about the issues. There are no prohibitions against communities calling on independent consultants to assist with these issues. I have seen politicians and law enforcement professionals imply that citizens were doing something "wrong" by bringing me in to solve their problems. The last time I checked the Constitution had not been changed. Citizens have the right to free speech and assembly.

The concept of community has been challenged by the lifestyle we live today. I felt very much a part of a community when I was growing up. As I mentioned earlier, everyone in the neighborhood knew everyone else and you could get help from a neighbor when needed. I recall that councilmen were not paid politicians but served only to represent their friends and neighbors in their part of town. Everyone's agenda was to make things better for the neighborhood. While we may not be able to change the physical structure of our present day communities, we do not have to lose the motivation, commitment, and drive that I witnessed so many years ago.

Criminals and drug dealers create tightly organized, highly disciplined and efficiently run business organizations. Their survival depends on total control of every level of their operation. Believe me; one thing I learned under cover is that an unorganized community with weak leaders is no match for the dedicated criminal. While the community is fighting and splintering into factions, the drug dealer has a singular focus to make as much money as possible by addicting as many people as possible as quickly as possible. Sadly, when most citizens think of drug dealers they see images of uneducated, street thugs. Nothing could be further from the truth. At the beginning of this book, I asked you to keep an open mind. Nowhere is that more necessary than here. If communities and the people elected to lead them do not change this one perception we don't have a chance. Citizens can succeed in turning out drug activity if they learn the right tools to do so. It all starts with realizing that each one of us have a responsibility to our community.

POPPY SEEDS, MYTHS & OTHER TRICKS

Beating the test::

I have been collecting drug test specimens for eleven years. You would think by now I would have experienced all the dopey things that dopers do to pass a drug test. People who use drugs have been called a lot of things, user is just one of many and they do just that. They use anything and anyone they can to get their next fix. They lie, cheat and steal to get high again. Here are some of the highlights from the past eleven years some funny, some sad and some scary..

The most common myth I hear is "I have a friend who failed their test because they ate poppy seeds.

So, if anything comes up, I want you to know I ate a poppy seed bagel this morning."Wow, how original. This tells me that they, like most of America, have seen the now infamous episode of an old TV sitcom or there is a very good chance that they are crossing their fingers and hoping they pass their drug test. The myth about poppy seeds could come true only under the most extreme of conditions. Perhaps if you are a three hundred pound person working in a bakery, gorging yourself on poppy seed baked goods all day long, your specimen may throw a red flag for opiates. Studies show that you would have to have the equivalent of a coffee cup full of pure poppy seeds to even have the possibility of any opiates show up in the specimen. Most often, once reviewed by the medical review officer, the findings are heroin use or excessive use of prescription products.

The second most common myth I hear is, "I went to the dentist this morning and they gave me extra Novocain. I was told that Novocain is refined cocaine." Most of those results turn out to be positive for cocaine use. Novocain and cocaine do not have the same identifiers that the labs are looking for.

Now, as you can imagine from reading this book, I don't embarrass easy. Yet, the third most common myth/excuse is when the donor says "I don't do drugs, but I had unprotected sex last night and my partner used drugs, so if anything shows up it is from the exchange of body fluids." Once I explain the likelihood of being positive by those means, the donor usually leaves or receives a positive result.

Next we deal with the intimidators. Earlier in this book, I said that the collector had to take charge and not allow him-self to be intimidated. Well, here's why. Let's start with the woman who sat at my desk, pulled a urine specimen from her purse and boldly informed me that I would take the substituted specimen and ignore the temperature otherwise she would ruin my career by ripping off her shirt and claiming I raped her. Luckily, the waiting room door was open and my office was, at that time, located in a very busy building. I was able to get her out of the office, without accepting the substitute urine and immediately called a security consultant. Two days later, I had security cameras in my office. Then there was the six foot five parolee who assured me that if he failed his test he would find out where I lived and deal with me appropriately as he pulled out his prepared specimen. I pointed to the cameras (thank you lady who wanted to accuse me of rape) and grabbed the phone to dial 911 as I wished him luck in finding someone he might be able to intimidate. I can get away with that because of my size. I strongly suggest to my employees and to the people I train that they take whatever steps necessary to avoid confrontation.

Intimidation comes in many forms and not always from the donor. Frequently, the business owner, HR professional or personnel in charge of drug test programs subtly suggest that I "turn my head" once in awhile or risk losing the account. This is in response to communities who don't have enough drug-free people to hire or the reluctance to fire friends, family and long time workers who can't pass a drug test.

Then there are the dopes that do dopey things. There was the Caucasian kid with a knitted hat full of dreadlocks. Part of the protocol is to ask donors to empty pockets, remove outerwear, coats, hats, etc. This young man was not about to remove that hat for any reason. The hair was part of the hat. Normally, I would excuse him and that would be the end of the conversation. This particular day, I just could not resist. As he was washing his hands prior to the collection I reached in and squeezed his hat. That's right, this dope had urine running down his face and neck. Have you ever laughed so hard you thought you were going to lose control of your bodily functions? I thought I would lose it for sure when he looked me in the eye and asked "Are you crazy what are you laughing at?" I replied "I am picturing you and me at the psychiatrist's office. Who do you think is getting the crazy certificate?"

Then there was the woman who was in the process of giving a specimen, when from outside the restroom I heard her mutter some foul language followed by what sounded like a slap. When she came out of the restroom, her shirt was drenched. The first urine filled condom she pulled from her bra broke, causing her to swear. In an attempt to catch it, she had slapped herself inadvertently breaking the second urine filled condom also lodged in her bra. And, of course, she insisted on a lengthy explanation of why her shirt was wet while the cup was empty. I tried to politely listen, but as the story got more ridiculous, I simply said "if you are not breast-feeding I am not interested in your story."

Next we have the guy who informed me that he would not be able to provide a urine specimen unless he was able to "do number two." Yes, this was an adult. I felt sorry for him as I heard his painful groans followed by much foul language and a horrible odor. He actually had "a number three." He urinated, defecated and, painfully, produced a tube filled with urine! My walls and floor were splattered with feces as his final push released the tube of urine hidden in his rectum. My immediate laughter turned into a sarcastic demand convincing him to thoroughly sanitize my bathroom before he left my facility. I believe I told him I don't give any s— and I certainly am not going to take any s—.

The most pathetic experience is the mother who tries everything to get her young child into the bathroom with her. Just recently, I had a young mother with her four year-old daughter come to my office. While preparing her paperwork, I developed a rapport with her daughter. She insisted that her daughter had to go into the restroom with her, stressing that once out of her sight, the child would be uncontrollable. After a short exchange, the child looked at her mother, saying, "It's, O.K., Mommy; I don't have to pee-pee for you right now." Most often, they just leave and cancel the test when they realize I am not going to allow the child into the restroom with them.

Who can forget the guy who smuggled the sub-stituted urine into the bathroom and after a few choice words, exited the restroom with a urine-soaked arm and pant leg. The lighter in his hand and plastic specimen cup with a hole burned through the bottom were a dead givea-way. Moral of this story is: Figure out the heat tolerance of the collection cup before you try to heat it to acceptable temperature by putting a lighter to it!

Another common way to bring substituted urine to body temperature is by strapping it to the engine of your car to keep it warm as you travel to the collection site. Pure genius! On more than one occasion, either by camera or the virtue of timing, I have witnessed donors popping the hood and trying not to burn themselves when trying to hide the overheated specimen.

The only thing dopier than watching that dance is the look on their face when you inform them that you witnessed the entire thing, followed by relief as they quickly dispose of the burning container. And now, as a favor to all these geniuses, let me set the record straight. Most engines will heat liquids to temperatures far in excess of normal human body temperature. (Do I even need to say animal body temperatures, too?)

A fellow collector shared the following incident with me. She was waiting for the donor to complete giving the specimen when she heard cries for help coming from the bathroom. Imagine her surprise when she found the young donor with his foot stuck in the toilet. Apparently, the young man had attempted to hide the containers that held the smuggled urine in the drop ceiling. This required standing on the toilet. Well, you guessed it. He lost his footing and ended up with his foot stuck in the toilet. She can't even tell this story without breaking into bouts of laughter.

There are hundreds of these scenarios and, after eleven years, I am certain that I have yet to see them all. So I'll end with my favorite little dope. While preparing a donor for the collection, part of the protocol is to ask the donor to display all items in his pockets. I try to keep it light so I usually say, "Can you please display all the items in your pockets. Do you have any cigarettes, lighters, powders, fluids, or anybody else's urine?" He looked at me and asked if his wife called as he pulled two vials of urine from his pocket. I replied, "No, but thank you I wasn't going to frisk you."

You would think that the conversation ends with these types of situations. But, in reality, they get far more amusing when the parent, spouse or significant other calls to explain why I possibly could not have experienced these events. I often joke about being a comedian after I retire. Sadly, there is no shortage of material.

PARTING
THOUGHTS

While it is my sincere hope that I have exposed the loopholes and trade secrets that undermine the drug and alcohol testing industry, I have also tried to present workable solutions. A drug free America can be a reality. It starts with each of us realizing that we, not politicians, law enforcement or government agencies, working-independent of us, can achieve what we have been taught to believe is the impossible. The purpose of writing this book was not to bash politicians and law enforcers, but to show how the system itself has prohibited fine individuals from doing their jobs effectively and on behalf of the country as a whole.

I have attempted to convey that drugs are not just a workplace problem or a school problem or a community problem. The drug user who goes undetected at work because of a poor or manipulated drug testing program brings his addiction home to his community. There, his children are negatively influenced and affected by this parent under the influence. The cost of his addiction in monies spent on drugs, time not spent with the children and the risk of detection and criminal consequences, not to mention the risk of killing innocent people on the job or road weighs heavily on the family. As a drug user, he is certainly not going to be part of any community activities that will deter hardened drug dealers and traffickers who rely on his addiction to prosper.

The intent of this book is to motivate readers to come back together, as we did in the 50's and before that, to solve issues with common sense for the common good not just for the immediate gratification and financial and political benefits of those who lead. If we can unite, behind this common goal, and remain focused on the real enemy which is drugs in our communities, workplaces and schools the economic, social and health benefits will be far reaching and long lasting.

I am an average person just like you. I am not a law-enforcement professional. However, I am an expert on law enforcement with nearly three decades of success in eradicating drug and criminal activity. As an ordinary citizen, I persisted until I found law enforcement agencies that would benefit from my personal agenda. Through that avenue, I was instrumental in causing the second largest organized crime trials in my community since the 1957 Apalachin gangland convention. Since then, I have been able to help countless families and neighborhoods eradicate drugs, crime and addiction issues. My efforts continue to redirect political and law enforcement agenda's to benefit potential victims of continued failed policies.

My challenge to you is to join me in living like an American instead of *dreaming* of living like an American. Join me in taking action in your schools, neighborhoods and communities. Arrange town meetings, neighborhood forums or debates. Invite your elected officials to answer the tough questions in public forums. Refuse to be silenced when your needs threaten the agendas of short-sighted self-serving public servants. If you desire help, you are invited to contact me.

I welcome the opportunity to sit down with or debate any public official about eradicating drug problems and have repeated that offer over and over again. So far, no politician or law enforcer has taken up the challenge. The people who profit from drugs will eventually have to come together if ordinary citizens join me in replicating my successes on a massive nationwide scale. What are you prepared to do? I am here. I am ready.

RESOURCES & REFERENCES

INTRODUCTION

THE FEDERAL DRUG AND ALCOHOL TESTING INDUSTRY

1.... Title V Omnibus Transportation
       Employee Testing
       Public Law 102-143 passed October 28,
       1991
       http://www.dot.gov/ost/dapc/
       frpubs/199111028_Omnibus_Act.pdf

2.... U.S. Department of Transportation
       http://www.dot.gov/ost/dapc/

3.... *legislative history of the Omnibus*
Transportation Employee Testing Act of 1991

Report of the Senate Committee on Commerce,
Science, and Transportation on S 676

Omnibus Transportation Employee Testing Act
of 1991 - April 9, 1991
http://www.dot.gov/ost/dapc/frpubs/
Congressional_Report_Omnibus_Act.pdf

4.... *January 4,1987 Conrail train wreck, Chase,*
Maryland
Article from, The Daily Intelligencer,
Doylestown, PA - January 5, 1987
http://www3.gendisasters.com/mary-
land/1720/essex%2C-md-amtrak-train-
collision%2C-jan-1987

5.... 49 CFR Part 40 Subpart A Section 40.1
http://www.dot.gov/ost/dapc/NEW_
DOCS/part40.html?proc

6.... Title V Omnibus Transportation
Employee Testing Public Law
102-143 passed October 28, 1991
http://www.dot.gov/ost/dapc/

frpubs/199111028_Omnibus_Act.pdf
http://www.dot.gov/ost/dapc/NEW_
DOCS/part40.html?proc

7.... 40 CFR Part 40 Subpart B Section 40.23
http://www.dot.gov/ost/dapc/NEW_
DOCS/part40.html?proc

8.... Urine Specimen Collections
49 CFR Part 40 Subpart E Section 40.61
(b) (1)

9.... Alcohol Screening Tests
49 CFR Part 40 Subpart L Section 40.241
(b) (1)

10.... Donor not allowed to leave testing area
during the process
49 CFR Part 40 Subpart E Section 40.63
(2) (e)

11.... Problems that always cause a drug test to
be cancelled
49 CFR part 40 Subpart I Section 40.199

12.... Problems that always cause a drug test to
be cancelled and may result in a

(Effective%20November%201,%202004).
pdf

18.... Preliminary steps in the collection process
49 CFR Part 40 Subpart E Section 40.61

19.... Required steps in the collection process
49 CFR Part 40 Subpart E Section 40.63

20.... Employers general responsibilities in the
collection process
49 CFR part 40 Subpart B Section 40.11 (b)

21.... New York State Public Health Law
Section 571 (1)

22.... Basic training requirements for collectors
49 CFR part 40 Subpart C Section 40.33

23.... Collectors must complete mock collections
49 CFR Part 40 Subpart C Section 40.33
(c) (1) (2)

24.... Collector must follow required steps in
the collection process
49 CFR Part 40 Subpart E Section 40.61

25.... www.dot.gov

26.... Supervisor Substance abuse awareness
training
49 CFR Part 382 Subpart F Section
382.603

27.... Michael Levine, *Deep Cover, The Inside
Story of How DEA Infighting, Incompetence,
and Subterfuge Lost Us the Biggest Battle of
the Drug War*
(Nebraska, iUniverse, Inc. 2000)
An Authors Guild Backinprint.com edi-
tion, originally published by
Delacorte Press, 1990

Michael Levine, *Fight Back How to Take
back Your Neighborhoods, Schools and Families
from the DRUG DEALERS* (New York:
Dell Publishing a Division of Bantam
Doubleday Dell Publishing Group,
Inc.,1991)

Michael Levine with Laura Kavanau-
Levine, *The Big White Lie, the Cia and
the Cocaine/Crack Epidemic* (New York,
Thunder's Mouth Press, 1993) Michael

Levine, *Fight Back* (Nebraska, iUniverse, Inc., 2006) An Authors Guild Backinprint. com edition; originally published by Dell Publishing, 1991

28.... Michael Levine, *Fight Back How to Take back Your Neighborhoods, Schools and Families from the DRUG DEALERS* (New York: Dell Publishing a Division of Bantam Doubleday Dell Publishing Group, Inc.,1991)

Michael Levine, *Fight Back* (Nebraska, iUniverse, Inc., 2006) An Authors Guild Backinprint.com edition; originally published by Dell Publishing, 1991

Websites

Substance Abuse and Mental Health Services Administration (SAMHSA)
www.samhsa.gov

Office of National Drug Control Policy
www.whitehousedrugpolicy.gov

National Institute on Drug Abuse (NIDA)
www.nida.nih.gov

GLOSSARY

The following terms are taken from 49 CFR Part 40 Section 40.3. This is not an exhaustive list. Please refer to Section 40.3 for additional terms

Adulterated Specimen: A specimen that contains a substance that is not expected to be present in human urine, or contains a substance expected to be present but is at a concentration so high that it is not consistent with human urine

Alcohol Confirmation Test: A subsequent test using an EBT, following a screening test with a result of 0.02 or greater, that provides quantitative data about the alcohol concentration

Alcohol Screening Test: An analytic procedure to determine whether an employee may have a prohibited concentration of alcohol in a breath or salvia specimen

Blind Specimen or Blind Performance Test Specimen: A specimen submitted to a laboratory for quality control testing purposes, with a fictitious identifier, so that the laboratory cannot distinguish it from an employee specimen

Breath Alcohol Technician (BAT): A person who instructs and assists employees in the alcohol testing process and operates an evidential breath testing device

Cancelled Test: A drug or alcohol test that has a problem that cannot be or has not been corrected or which this part otherwise requires to be cancelled. A cancelled test is neither a positive nor a negative test

Chain of Custody: The procedure used to document the handling of the urine specimen from the time the employee gives the specimen to the collector until the specimen is destroyed. This procedure uses the Federal Drug Testing Custody and Control Form (CCF)

Collector: A person who instructs and assists employees at a collection site, who receives and makes an initial inspection of the specimen provided by those employees, and who initiates and completes the CCF

Confirmation (or confirmatory) Drug Test: A second analytical procedure performed on a urine specimen to identify and quantify the presence of a specific drug or drug metabolite

Confirmed Drug Test: A confirmation test result received by an MRO from a laboratory

Consortium/Third Party Administrator (C/TPA): A service agent that provides or coordinates the provision of a variety of drug and alcohol testing services to employers. C/TPAs typically perform administrative tasks concerning the operation of the employers' drug and alcohol testing programs. This term includes, but is not limited to, groups of employers who join together to administer, as a single entity, the DOT drug and alcohol testing programs of its members. C/TPAs are not "employers" for purposes of this part.

Designated Employer Representative (DER): An employee authorized by the employer to take immediate action(s) to remove employees from safety-sensitive duties, or cause employees to be removed from these covered duties, and to make required decisions in the testing and evaluation processes. The DER also receives test results and other communication for the employer, consistent with the requirements of this part. Service agents cannot act as DERs.

Dilute Specimen: A specimen with creatinine and specific gravity values that are lower than expected for human urine

DOT, Department Transportation, The DOT agency: These terms encompass all DOT agencies, including, but not limited to, the United States Coast Guard (USCG), The Federal Aviation Administration (FAA), the Federal Railroad Administration (FRA), The Federal Motor Carrier Safety Administration (FMCSA), the Federal Transit Administration (FTA), the National Highway Traffic Safety Administration (NHTSA), the Research and Special Programs Administration (RSPA), and the Office of the

Secretary (OST). These terms include any designee of a DOT agency.

Drugs: The drugs for which tests are required under this part and the DOT agency regulations are marijuana, cocaine, amphetamines, phencyclidine (PCPO and opiates)

Employee: Any person who is designated in a DOT agency regulation as subject to drug testing and/or alcohol testing. The term includes individuals currently performing safety-sensitive functions designed in DOT agency regulations and applicants for employment subject to pre-employment testing. For purposes of drug testing under this part, the term employee has the same meaning as the term "donor" as found on CCF and related guidance materials produced by the department of Health and Human Services.

Employer: A person or entity employing one or more employees (including an individual who is self employed) subject to DOT agency regulations requiring compliance with this part. The term includes an employer's officers, representatives, and management personnel. Service agents are not employers for the purposes of this part

Evidential Breath Testing Device (EBT): A device approved by NHTSA for the evidential testing of breath at the .02 and .04 alcohol concentrations, placed on NHTSA's conforming products list (CPL) for "Evidential Breath Measurement Devices" and identified on the CPL as conforming with the model specifications available from NHTSA's Traffic Safety Program

HHS: The Department of Health and Human Services or any designeee of the Secretary, Department of Health and Human Services

Initial Drug Test: The test used to differentiate a negative specimen from one that requires further testing for drugs or drug metabolites.

Invalid Drug Test: The result of a drug test for a urine specimen that contains an unidentified adulterant or an unidentified interfering substance, has abnormal physical characteristics, or has an endogenous substance at an abnormal concentration that prevents the laboratory from completing or obtaining a valid drug test result.

Laboratory: Any U.S. laboratory certified by HHS under the National Laboratory Certification

Program as meeting the minimum standards of Subpart C of JJS Mandatory Guidelines for Federal Workplace Drug Testing Programs; or, in the case of foreign laboratories, a laboratory approved for participation by DOT under this part. (The HHS Mandatory Guidelines for Federal Workplace Drug Testing Programs are available on the Internet at http://www.health.org/workplace/ or from the Division of Workplace Programs

Medical Review Officer (MRO): A person who is a licensed physician and who is responsible for receiving and reviewing laboratory results generated by an employer's drug testing program and evaluating medical explanations for certain drug test results.

Office of Drug and Alcohol Policy and Compliance (ODAPC): An office in the Office of the Secretary, DOT, that is responsible for coordinating drug and alcohol testing program matters within the department and providing information concerning the implementation of this part.

Primary Specimen: In drug testing, the urine specimen bottle that is opened and tested by a first laboratory to determine whether the employee has a drug or drug metabolite in his or her system; and for the purpose of validity testing. The primary specimen is distinguished from the split specimen, defined in this section.

Qualification Training: The training required in order for a collector, BAT, MRO, SAP or STT to be qualified to perform their function in the DOT drug and alcohol testing program. Qualification training may be provided by any appropriate means

(e.g., classroom instruction, Internet application, CD-ROM, video)

Refresher Training: The training required periodically for qualified collectors, BATs, and STTs to review basic requirements and provide instruction concerning changes in technology (e.g., new testing methods that may be authorized) and amendments, interpretations, guidance and issues concerning this part and DOT agency drug and alcohol testing regulations. Refresher training can be provided by any appropriate means (e.g. classroom instruction, internet application, CD-ROM, video).

Service Agent: Any person or entity, other than an employee of the employer, who provides services specified under this part to employers and/or employees in connection with DOT drug and alcohol testing requirements. This includes but is not limited to collectors, BATs and STTs, laboratories, MROs, substance abuse professionals, and C/TPAs. To act as service agents, persons and organizations must meet the qualifications set forth in applicable sections of this part. Service agents are not employers for purposes of this part.

Screen Test Technician (STT): conducts only alcohol screening tests, but a BAT can conduct alcohol screening and confirmation test.

Specimen Bottle: The bottle that, after being sealed and labeled according to the procedures in this part, is used to hold the urine specimen during transportation to the laboratory.

Split Specimen: In drug testing, a part of the urine specimen that is sent to a first laboratory and retained unopened, and which is transported to a second laboratory in the event that the employee requests that it be tested following a verified positive test of the primary specimen or a verified adulterated or substituted test result.

Substance Abuse Professional (SAP): A person who evaluates employees who have violated a DOT drug and alcohol regulation and makes recommendations concerning education, treatment, follow-up testing, and aftercare.

Substituted Specimen: A specimen with creatinine and specific gravity values that are so diminished that they are not consistent with human urine.

Verified Test: A drug test result or validity testing result from an HHS-certified laboratory that has undergone review and final determination by the MRO.

FIGHT BACK

A Solution Between Prohibition and Legalization
By: Michael Levine

This essay appears in the book *After Prohibition: an adult approach to drug policies in the 21 Century by* LYNCH, TIMOTHY Copyright: 2000 Reproduced with permission of CATO INSTITUTE in the format Other book via Copyright Clearance Center

> **"The effort expended by the bureaucracy in defending any error is in direct proportion to the size of the error." - John Nies**

As we approach the new millennium, the now 30 year, trillion dollar war on drugs, despite overwhelming evidence of its failure—from treatment on demand and interdiction programs to its street law enforcement and billion dollar ad campaigns— still grinds onward with even bigger budgets, wreaking even more havoc on our Constitution and filling our jails with more people than populate some entire countries. To say the least, it's time to try something new. If there is such a thing as the fruits of a 35 year career as an international federal narcotic officer, trial consultant and expert witness, then they are found in a program which I developed called The Fight Back Community-Police Anti Drug Partnership.

Someone once said that all new ideas begin as heresy. However, Fight Back, when first presented in a book published in 1991, was well received. The plan was reviewed by the Swedish Carnegie Institute as "the only drug plan ever to come out of America that made any sense." It was recommended reading for communities with drug problems by the Clinton Drug Policy Office in 1993. In fact, it showed promise of solving much of our nation's drug problems, sharply reducing police corruption and brutality as well as greatly increasing police-community harmony. So why, in eight years, has this promising program not even been given a trial run? Understanding the Fight Back system, how the idea was conceived and the nature of the obstacles placed in the path of even a modest trial run, casts a revealing light on the real reasons why this failed drug war still continues in full force.

To fully understand the evolution of Fight Back, it is important to understand both my personal and professional stake in our national drug problem. In the mid 1980's when the idea first came to me, I had already compiled more than twenty years as a federal narcotic agent. In that time I was directly credited with more than 3,000 arrests and the seizure of several tons of illegal drugs. As a supervisory agent I had overseen at least four times those numbers. I had accomplished all of our nations ultimate drug war goals, in that I had engineered the highest level sting operations which successfully penetrated the major drug producing cartels in the world. Yet as all of us who took part in these operations observed, all that we had done at the cost of our lives and families had no effect whatsoever on the streets of the nation we had taken an oath to serve and protect.

A series of deep cover cases in the 1980's had placed me, posing undercover as a top level Mafia don, face to face with the very people controlling a major part of all the raw cocaine produced at that time, *La Mafia Cruzeña* —the Bolivian cocaine cartel—the suppliers of all the materials the Colombian Cartels converted to cocaine. I learned that not only did they have no fear of our war on drugs, they counted on it to increase market price and to weed out the smaller, inefficient drug dealers. They found US interdiction efforts laughable. The only US action they feared was an effective demand reduction program. On one undercover tape-recorded conversation, a top cartel chief, Jorge Roman, expressed his gratitude for the drug war, calling it "a sham put on for the American taxpayer" that was actually "good for business."

Even more dismaying was when I reported Roman's statements to the DEA officer in command of Operation Snowcap— the paramilitary operations begun in South America which Attorney General Edwin Meece had promised would reduce the flow of cocaine to America by sixty percent in three years— he sided with the drug trafficker stating, "We know [the military operations] don't work, but we sold the plan up and down the Potomac...[Snowcap] is going to succeed, one way or the other, or DEA goes down the tubes."

My involvement with family drug problems, if anything, was even more intense than my career exposure. After twenty years on the front lines of the drug war, I was reassigned to New York City as the supervisor of a street enforcement group, as a result of a compassionate transfer granted me by DEA due to my 15 year old daughter's cocaine addiction. My brother David, a heroin addict for 19 years and graduate of six government funded treatment-on-demand programs had already committed suicide in Miami, leaving a note stating "I am sorry...I can't stand the drugs any longer."

Terrified that my daughter might go the same way as my brother I was determined to do whatever it took to save her. And now there was a new worry. My son Keith Richard Levine had just become a New York City police officer and on his very first night of duty had, in a drug related incident, come chillingly close to death. A few years later my boy's luck would run out— he was killed in the line of duty by a lifelong drug addict who, like my brother, had been vetted through numerous treatment-on-demand programs. The man, free on parole, had been convicted of two homicides prior to killing my son.

And it wasn't just my family. During my career I had watched our federal drug war budget go from tens of millions to tens of billions, yet the problem throughout the US was worse than ever. I was coming to the end of my career and I was plagued with the notion that it had all been for nothing. With all the expertise I had acquired, could I not at least find a viable solution before I retired?

The 92nd Street Drug War Blitz—A Typical Failure

If I had to pick the specific moment when the Fight Back program began to take shape, it was probably on a warm spring evening on the Upper West Side of Manhattan. I sat in a black Mercedes sedan, seized months earlier from a drug dealer, with the engine running to keep the A/C going and the salsa music pulsing low and steady.

When the guy with the baseball cap knocked on the passenger side window I jumped, startled. I'd been watching the street corner behind me, 92nd Street and Amsterdam Avenue, through my rearview, thinking about the battle that was about to take place there. Months earlier, in drug related incidents, two young cops had been killed on the same night only a few blocks away. One was killed while making an undercover street buy of cocaine, just as I was about to do. My UC buy was to be the opening salvo of a high intensity drug enforcement operation begun by the 92nd Street Block Association, a politically active, multi-racial organization of middle to upper income professionals.

As one of the association's leaders whom I will call "Vernon" described, the intersection, the very heart of their community, was taken over by drug dealers as soon as the sun went down. Area residents became frightened, cowering victims in high rise caves, fearful of even going to the local stores for milk. Years of conventional police action had accomplished nothing. Vernon had contacted Congressman Charles Rangel. The group paid more than its share of drug war taxes, couldn't anything be done?

Congressman Rangel responded by applying political pressure and demanding action from DEA. That's where I came in. I was placed in charge of a 25 man task force of DEA agents and city detectives. My orders: "Clean up that damned corner, once and for all."

We were able to identify more than 100 probable street dealers within 50 feet of the intersection, servicing an endless flow of customers from dusk till dawn. My agents also learned that the during the past several years the local police had made hundreds of dealer arrests on the intersection, yet our eyes didn't lie: business could not have been better.

Rudolph Giuliani, the then US Attorney, assigned one of his assistants to oversee the operation. It was easily decided that the arrests of the dealers would have to be done on the basis of simple observations of what appeared to be illegal drug sales—Probable Cause. We did not have the manpower to use the traditional investigative measures of undercover buys backed up by surveillance and field investigation which would have made a successful prosecution in court more likely. In order to target that many potential dealers for arrest, adhering to constitutional and legal safeguards insuring due process, would have required hundreds of man hours to arrest a single dealer and thousands to convict him. I would have needed 1,000 officers to police that one single corner and there were only 250 DEA agents stationed in New York at the time.

This was a typical example of what every professional narcotic officer learns during his or her career but is reluctant say in public: there is a simple numeric equation that shows clearly that enforcing criminal laws against dealers has about as much chance of making any impact on the drug problem as breaking the sound barrier with your Honda Civic.

Here's the equation: Number of Potential Drug Dealers - *plus* - World's Potential Source Countries -*divided by* - Number of Narcotic Officers & Available Budget -*multiplied by* - Constitutional Legal Process to Arrest and/or Seize -*equals:* Total Absurdity of US Drug War Policy.

But the prosecutor did insist that the first arrest of the operation be made in the conventional way—an undercover buy/bust—for a good legal reason. A new federal law had just been passed making the sale of drugs within 1,000 feet of a school a "super felony" with a minimum manda-tory sentence. This was to be its first prosecution in Manhattan. Giuliani, wanting to make certain that he had a winner and that a message be sent to other dealers, ordered that the undercover agent making the first buy be able to testify that the dealer knew, beyond a reasonable doubt, that he was selling drugs near a school.

Since I was fluent in Spanish—most of the deal-ers were Dominicans— I decided to do make the buy myself to try and get an idea of how the deal-ers thought about the new law. And what better way to prove that the dealer was aware that he was selling dope near a school than to do the transaction parked directly under one of the new signs screaming: DRUG FREE, SCHOOL ZONE. You got the money?" he says getting into my car, showing me a package of white powder. He's a good looking young Dominican kid, early twen-ties, alert eyes darting all over the street catching every movement.

I read him as typical of the wave young Dominican "Illegal's" coming to New York City to make their fortune selling cocaine and returning to their country where they buy homes and businesses, marry their childhood sweethearts and become honored men. The hypocrisy of our drug war— our covert support of drug dealing political allies and our elected leaders violating the same laws for which our citizens are serving jail time— has made coming to America and getting rich in the drug market, in the view of Third World youth, an almost mythical rite of passage. An honorable adventure.

The bag of dope is in his left hand extended toward me, his right hand is out of sight. He's waiting for the money and he doesn't have much patience. Without a word I point to the **DRUG FREE SCHOOL ZONE** sign, right above the windshield.

The guy laughs and waves his finger at me, "Hey, that don't mean you get the coke for free." I laugh too, hand him the money and hit my blinkers— the signal for his arrest. He's counting money and doesn't see the guys closing in with guns in their hands.

Sometimes people laugh when I tell the story, but there's nothing funny about it. The law meant less than nothing to the dealer. If the history of the drug war has shown us anything, it is that no matter how Draconian the law, drug dealers are not impressed. They have proven themselves, time and again, willing to risk jail and even death for the money. And as every dealer knows, if he is arrested there are hundreds right behind him ready to take his place. The money is just too good. And like the human wave attacks during the Korean war, their sheer numbers, in spite of all laws, have long overtaxed our resources.

It took a squad of 10 men the rest of the night to process the prisoner, run down some leads, write reports, store evidence, seize and inventory his car, question and release for lack of evidence two people who had accompanied him and store him in a cell at the MCC. By the following morning we had expended approximately 220 total man hours on the case and much of the administrative work including case reports were still to be done.. The doper was free on bail before we could get home to sleep and has never been seen since. He's joined the huge and growing legion of drug war fugitives that, if all were caught, would now require a prison the size of Rhode Island to house.

Drug Possession Arrests—A Misunderstood Statistic — a False Conclusion

One of the most important lessons to be learned from the 92nd Street Operation came during the dealer arrest stage. Within two weeks my task force had made close to 80 dealer arrests, most of which were made on the basis of observations alone. This meant that proving sale of drugs in court was virtually impossible. A lawyer from 1-800 AMBULANCE CHASER could get an innocent verdict and we all knew it. Thus most of the arrested dealers were only charged with Possession.

Of the 10,000 plus narcotic investigations that I have been associated with during my career, 99 percent targeted dealers—not buyers. However, most arrested dealers were either charged with, or plea bargained for a Possession violation because it is simply a legal expedient that saves time and court costs.

Now the reason I mention this important fact is that I have heard many experts state that since the highest percentage of jailed drug cases results from Possession arrests, the US drug war is therefore a "war on drug users." The reason drug war bureaucrats and politicians usually don't even respond to this accusation is that it could not be further from the truth, yet the notion persists. Many of the drug war bureaucrats are actually happy to hear the false claim repeated over and over in media, because it acts to discredit much of the otherwise credible drug war opposition and to maintain the status quo. In fact, an interesting statistic proves my point: according to DEA 85 percent of drug consumers are white. My personal experience indicates that figure to be closer to 90 percent. If the drug war was truly being waged against consumers, these statistics would be reflected in jail populations, but as we all know—they are not.

Some experts also continue to misunderstand the racially unbalanced jail populations of those incarcerated for drug violations, making a blanket claim that the drug war somehow targets minorities instead of whites. While recognizing that unfortunately racism does exist in law enforcement as it does in much of today's society, those of us on the inside of narcotic enforcement know that this is not the predominant reason for the disparity in jail population. Rather, it is more directly connected to our philosophy of focusing the majority of our law enforcement efforts on arresting suppliers and dealers, the majority of whom happen to be minorities for a combination of economic, linguistic and cultural reasons combined with ill advised immigration policies.

The 92nd Street campaign turned out to be typical of street narcotic enforcement in urban America. For a couple of days we succeeded in sharply reducing the appearance of a drug market, mainly because the police activity frightened off the buyers; however, within a week of our departure "Vernon" called me with bad news. The drug dealers, in many cases the same people whom we had arrested were on the street selling again. It was as if we had never even been there. The father of two preteen daughters was at his wits end. "If all those cops and agents couldn't get this one corner clean, what is the purpose of this whole damned drug war?" he asked. "You're a DEA agent; can you explain it to me?" I was as desperate for an answer as he was.

The Drug War Is An Obvious Failure, So Why Does it Continue?

I began to do something I had never done before in my career: examine the mechanics of our war on drugs and the motivation of those pursuing it, including my own. I used classic investigative reasoning, asking the question: Who benefits most from a continued war on drugs?

I found a quote by Brooks Atkinson that seemed to resonate: "Bureaucracies are designed to perform public business. But as soon as a bureaucracy is established, it develops an autonomous spiritual life and comes to regard the public as its enemy."

The trillion dollar war on drugs then included 53 federal, military, law enforcement and covert agencies, the Partnership for a Drug Free America and all its branches, treatment-on-demand programs —just for starters. This wasn't even counting state agencies that came under separate budgets like New York State which, under Governor Cuomo's watch at the time, had its own drug war budget of one billion dollars. It brought to mind how DEA agents would joke whenever mainstream media would headline some new statistic showing that we were winning: "Please! Not yet," someone would cry. "I've got a mortgage to pay." One DEA Administrator in response to media trumpeted claims, used to address audiences of agents with "I guess we've 'turned the corner' again." Some agent would always respond: "Yeah, we've squared the block."

The point is that none of these bureaucracies even consider the possibility of successfully completing their goals. On the contrary they all vie with each other for bigger cases, headlines and media exposure which translate down to a bigger cut of the budget, more money, more authority and more power. The notion of really winning a drug war is so far out of the question that anyone who even mentions it is considered some kind of a nut. Perhaps there are some individuals who sincerely wish for that victory to come, but nobody really believes it's possible. And to say publicly what is secretly felt by every insider— that if the federal war on drugs were disbanded tomorrow it would make little difference on any street in America—is like invoking the Anti-Christ. It is a threat to the existence of the bureaucracy, to countless careers, benefits, money and security.

Mainstream Media: A Key Beneficiary of the Drug War.

The Fourth Estate, the national news media, which our founding fathers referred to as absolutely necessary to safeguard our Democracy must shoulder their share of the responsibility. The majority of us cannot accept that the drug war a complete failure mainly because mainstream media has done such a powerful job of selling it to us for decades and continues to do so.

The manipulation of media by bureaucrats to sell a failed, inept government policy is nothing new. For example, it is now evident that, through much of the buildup of the Vietnam war, mainstream media, with just a few exceptions, dutifully headlined the false intelligence estimates, battle statistics and body counts announced by our political and military leaders, without a minimal amount of investigation. This false information blitz kept us bleeding, dying and paying for a promised victory that never came. The media then painted all those insiders who tried to tell the truth with the pejorative "whistleblower," or worse, as anti-American. For too many years it convinced a majority of us, including me, at the time a young federal agent working undercover in Southeast Asia, to pay no attention to mounting evidence of the lies of our military and political leaders appearing in alternative media. If it's not in the *New York Times* it can't be true, can it?

Ironically, the drug war is now running an exact parallel to our Vietnam experience. In fact our military involvement in places like Bolivia, Colombia and Peru, under the banner of War on Drugs, continues to be increasingly funded and expanded to the point that some members of Congress have recently described them as leading us into "another Vietnam-type debacle." Yet mainstream media continues to respond to the manipulation of bureaucrats by ignoring this frightening forecast.

Throughout my career I have observed and, regrettably, took part in what can only be described as the ongoing unhealthy alliance between drug war and mainstream media bureaucracies. While stationed in New York City, for example, all the major networks and newspapers would call the DEA Special Agent in Charge when, due to a slow news week, they *needed* a drug story for ratings or to sell newspapers. The SAC was eager to comply because the request was always beneficial to the agency's image and budget, not to mention his own career. Dramatic raids in media, like the best in Madison Avenue advertising, sell the drug war. My unit, a very active street enforcement group, was often called on to plan drug raids for mainstream media cameras. Often, this would entail the disruption of undeveloped investigations to meet a media deadline and, at times, the use of dangerous and unprofessional tactics for dramatic effect, as happened with ATF's infamous Waco raid.

Of course, a kind of "don't ask" policy was in effect wherein the journalists involved would never ask an embarrassing question of the agency. But one must consider that they had to be hopelessly naive to accept at face value that DEA, FBI, ATF or any of the other drug war bureaucracies they approached for a story, just happened to have a dramatic, action-filled case ready to be filmed in time for their deadline.

If a particular journalist dared to question the veracity of what was happening, the next time he came to the agency for a story he'd run into a brick wall. He was getting nothing. Thus if a network or newspaper journalist wants continued access to any federal agency, they had better be friendly.

An example of this on an international scale came during the heat of the 1992 Presidential campaign. "Operation Green Ice" was called the biggest international money-laundering case in history, by every major media outlet in America. While it was being featured on everything from *Larry King Live* to *Geraldo*, I was getting angry calls from Customs and DEA agents who actually participated in the case.

The frustrated and enraged federal agents, who knew I would protect their identities, told me that the case was a fraud. The White House, through the Justice Department, had ordered Customs and DEA to come up with a series of major international arrests to "prove" that the Administration was making drug war "gains." Thus, many agents were ordered to prematurely shut down major money-laundering investigations so that their individual cases could be falsely included in a world-wide, headline grabbing roundup called "Operation Green Ice." It would be described by American politicians through an ever compliant media as "the best example of international cooperation" in the drug war, when, in fact, according to my sources, it was nothing more than a hodgepodge of hastily drawn indictments and unrelated arrest warrants linked together in an international drug conspiracy that never existed.

Ironically, I had just been invited to make a presentation in Paris by the French Government sponsored Geopolitical Drug Watch. Phillippe Bordes, a French journalist, approached me. He wanted to talk about, of all things, "Operation Green Ice." What did I think of it? He told me that French police had refused to take part in it, calling it an "obvious fraud." French law enforcement officials warned that if the American Justice Department persisted in trying to include them, they would blow the whistle on them in the French media.

Media Drug Money?

Perhaps the worst example of this mutual vested interest in a continued drug war between the bureaucracies and mainstream media happened in November 1998, when President Clinton and Newt Gingrich raised each other's bipartisan hands in "victory" and awarded an unprecedented $2 billion to mainstream media for yet another anti-drug ad campaign, making the Partnership for a Drug Free America the biggest advertiser on Madison Avenue.

In my book *Fight Back,* published in 1991, I had detailed research indicating that these same types of ads were not only ineffective but that there was much evidence indicating that they were counter-productive, and, further, that this sentiment was echoed by many educators across the land. *Brand Week,* the leading advertising trade magazine in a scathing commentary against this costly ad campaign, called it "suspect." Yet mainstream media had no comment. A cynical ex federal agent might conclude: Why would they comment when they are the recipients?

I was seated at a movie theater recently when one of these expensively produced, anti-drug ads was shown before the feature presentation—a Disney Studios release. It featured the story of a young black boy named "Kevin" who was forced to run home over back yard fences to escape the drug dealers, whom the narrator said, "would not take 'no' for an answer." The trouble with this message is that, as every kid knows, and as a Reagan Administration survey proved, virtually 100 percent of kids get their first hard drug experience *free* from their friends—it's called peer pressure.

Teenagers in the theater snickered at the million dollar plus ad. What the kids know apparently a lot better than the Partnership for a Drug Free

America who produced it, is that drug dealers don't come looking for customers, it is the other way around. And, as the article in *Brand Week* pointed out, Disney Studios was the recipient of the first $60 million of taxpayer funded ad money.

In the August 29th edition of the *New York Times,* for example, there was a full page, $50,000 ad, again, sponsored by the Partnership for a Drug Free America, called "How to Plan a Funeral For Your 12 Year Old Son" that almost drove *me* to drugs. The offensive ad ended with "If you don't want to learn about funerals learn about sniffing," as if anyone really believed that this keep a single kid off drugs. What really hurts is that there are effective and severely underfunded community groups that are successfully saving lives who could have used this $50,000 to fund their activities for many years.

The real irony about this $2 billion anti-drug media blitz came when I received a phone call from a frustrated DEA agent who still believed that stopping supply was the solution. Beside himself, he told me that according to DEA's own statistics, the money could have been used to purchase every single coca leaf grown in South America for that year, and some.

Unfortunately it was no surprise to me that *USA Today*, in its August 16, 1999 edition, published front page headlines trumpeting a statistical decrease in the use of drugs as "turning the corner," —an indication that the $2 billion ad campaign was money well spent. How could this be honest reporting when they failed to mention that precisely this same statistical victory claim had been repeated periodically for three decades? In fact, if they checked their own archives they would find that Drug Czar William Bennett retired in "victory" eight years ago on the wings of just such a claim. Recently, as happens often, a mainstream media journalist contacted me for a comment on a breaking story about the Mexican Drug war. Apparently he had uncovered even more evidence of Mexican government drug corruption constituting, as he said, "a serious threat to America."

He had no comment when I pointed out that our Congress had just granted Mexico "cooperating nation" status in the drug war. I told him that if he looked back over the past twenty-five years in the archives of his own newspaper, he would find the same pro forma, Mexican Drug War story printed almost bimonthly, the only thing that changed were the names of the various Mexican

Dr. Evils, amounts and dates. The syntax, adjectives and text were the same. He was writing a fill-in-the-blanks drug story. He didn't need an opinion, just a Xerox machine.

Incredible as it seems, I have documented the same formula drug stories printed across American newspaper headlines dating back eighty years. What mainstream media does not seem to realize, or does not want to realize, is that while the repetitious drug war "victory" headlines may sell newspapers and get ratings points, it also sells a deadly and wasteful drug war to a too gullible American public. If the Fourth Estate won't tell America that it's drug war is broken beyond all repair, who will?

But the really big question that remains is: If by some miracle we can get the nation to agree that the war on drugs is a failure—do we have a viable alternative solution to our drug problem?

Legalization, a Solution?

As most of us with first-hand experience with hard drugs believe, blanket legalization is more a threat to our nation than a solution. Especially to those of us who have loved ones at risk of addiction. Certain soft drugs may be legalized with a downside no worse than alcohol, but I am convinced that the hard stuff like crack, coke, heroin, angel dust, methamphetamine, LSD, ecstacy and dozens of others, simply cannot be legalized in a sane society.

A poll taken by the Bush Administration indicated that more than ninety percent of those children who grow up in ghettos and whom, through some miracle of will power, resist peer pressure and never take hard drugs, gave as their first reason for resisting, that drugs are *illegal.* Tell the father of one of these young heroes that you want to make hard drugs legal and watch out you don't get punched in the face.

Hard drugs, in my long experience, are relentlessly addictive and life-destroying, while alcohol, as damaging as it is in a small percentage of its buyers, is a long accepted rite of passage that is in most cases survivable. And while Peter Bourne, President Carter's Drug Advisor was proclaiming cocaine "the most benign of the illegal drugs," Michael Baden, New York City's Medical Examiner was pointing out before an audience of DEA agents and New York City Detectives, that "Cocaine, 80 percent of our hard-core drug problem, is a poison that kills directly by attacking every vital organ of the body." Only streetwise narcotic officers heard Dr. Baden's words, while the world media trumpeted the false proclamation of the White House drug expert.

Not only is there no real comparison between hard drugs and alcohol but the majority of our society does not want hard drugs legalized and have said so loud and clear in every poll—for good reason.

What happened in Russian society during the past decade seems to emphasize the point. Before Glasnost, when the use of hard drugs was a serious criminal offense, Russia maintained a hard-core addict population of less than 110,000. As a result of Glasnost the use of drugs was decriminalized. It is expected now that by the year 2,000 Russia will have more than 7 million hard-core addicts.

Even the experts, who call for blanket legalization, do not have convincing answers for obvious questions such as: How would you handle the sale and/or distribution of drugs like crack now estimated to be responsible for 60 percent of all crime? Angel dust? Heroin? LSD? Who would be allowed to sell and/or distribute hard drugs and to whom? How would prices be regulated? What about advertising campaigns? Would there be an age cut off? And if there is an age cut off, who would enforce those laws and how? If we gave away drugs like crack, cocaine and heroin free of charge, would the addicts then stop committing crimes to support themselves? What could a strung out crack addict who needs to toot up every 15 minutes do for a living? What do we do with the projected increase in crack babies? Is it not proven that some of these drugs, like crack, are in themselves violence inducing? Since we know that cocaine is a poison in itself, how do we handle the massive increase in medical costs? What about tobacco style law suits against the manufacturers of hard drugs?

The usual answers show that not much thought had been given toward the reality of what would actually happen in our society. Most experts seem to support legalization in its abstract. The fact is, blanket legalization creates as many problems as it solves.

And the latest paradox I have noticed is that many of the same people calling for the legalization of hard drugs are now calling for the prohibition of tobacco. Go figure.

What about Treatment as Solution?

There are two kinds of treatment—Treatment on Demand and Mandatory Treatment. Virtually all funding goes toward Treatment on Demand. I have never seen the question of the efficacy of Treatment on Demand answered more directly and with more impact than in a *Washington Post* article entitled "Treatment on Demand: The Mythology" by Richard Moran, a professor of Sociology and Criminology at Mount Holyoke College.

Professor Moran pointed out that in spite of their already being 1.4 million, taxpayer-paid, Treatment-on-Demand slots available for hard-core addicts, the Clinton Administration was about to spend $335 million to create an additional 140,000 slots, and that all of it was doomed to fail since the whole theory of "Treatment-on-Demand" is based on three unproved and highly doubtful assumptions:

"Assumption 1: That heavy drug buyers want to be treated. Unfortunately this assumption goes against the weight of evidence. Despite the constant increase of "Treatment on Demand" programs, the number of hard-core addicts, 2.7 million, has remained constant for 15 years. A national Institute of Drug Abuse study on the spread of HIV found that almost half of all drug addicts who had been on hard drugs for more than fifteen years had never been on any treatment whatsoever, not even detoxification. For them the dreadful reality is that drug addiction is a way of life that no political rhetoric, pleading or ad campaign will ever change.

"Assumption 2: That drug treatment is not available. The 1.4 million slots already available, using the average residential program length of nine months would indicate that all known addicts could undergo treatment within an 18 month period. Professor Moran pointed out that there were long waiting lists "here and there, and needs and available programs do not always coincide. Nonetheless, most programs still operate below capacity. An addict who requests treatment is often on as many as 10 waiting lists, thus creating the mistaken impression that drug addicts are clamoring to get into current treatment programs.

"The truth is that many addicts...have been in and out of treatment all their lives. In a Western Massachusetts drug detoxification clinic, for example, the average addict has been treated more than 200 times." My own brother had been through at least six treatment programs.

"Assumption 3: Treatment is effective in eliminating long-term drug use. As professor Moran concluded, the statistics show that hard-core addiction is "all but impossible to treat, and certainly not on an 'on-demand' basis. Indeed research from the National Institute of Drug Abuse Study suggests that hard-core drug addiction runs its course in about 15 years, whether or not treatment is provided. Without adequate knowledge of how to treat heavy drug buyers, adding more treatment slots will turn out to be a colossal waste of time and money."

Given that Treatment on Demand programs are a statistically proven failure, it is sobering to note that whole massive treatment bureaucracies and industries, depending on a steady flow of addicts for their income, have now proliferated throughout the US. The last I heard, for example, was that the director of Phoenix House, one of the largest, non-profit, Treatment on Demand programs in the US, himself an ex addict, was earning a salary in the high six figures. It should therefore be no surprise to anyone that when I began my research on the Fight Back program and interviewed a woman answering a cocaine hotline; she confided that she had been told by her supervisors that every incoming call is a potential $17,000.

Are There Solutions That We Have Not Tried Yet?

I found the first clue leading me toward the Fight Back solution in a statement made in 1975 by Congressman Charles Rangel on the floor of Congress: "...when the People's Republic of China eradicated...[its drug addiction problem]...the United States took no notice of that significant fact. This was a reflection of our foreign policy of pretending that they did not even exist..."

Those words started me on an incredible journey of discovery that continues to this day. I like most

Americans believed that China solved its massive drug problem by executing all the people who wouldn't quit. In fact, that is what I still hear experts telling Americans to this day. Yet, when I researched the facts I was astounded to find out that this too, like the arrest and treatment statistics, could not have been farther from the truth.

Chinese Cure

As I eventually detailed in my book *Fight Back,* I learned that at the end of World War II, China had a staggering 70 million heroin and opium addicts. In 1949 when Mao Tse-Tung's army conquered mainland China, he made his first priority the suppression of *drug addiction*— not a war against drug supply or dealers.

All hard-core addicts were required to undergo mandatory treatment, or be forcibly interned in a treatment center until cured. The program was accompanied by an anti drug *consumer* propaganda program. The consumer was depicted as the real enemy of Chinese society, the culprit who fueled the drug economy without whom there would be no supply problem. An enemy yes, but a redeemable one who could only reinvent himself by rehabilitation. In other words

Chinese society was going to save and redeem the addicts whether they liked it or not.

The result of the program was that by spring of 1951, less than two years after its inception, the New China News Agency was able to announce that China's drug problem of 70 million addicts was "fundamentally eradicated." Compare this with the 2.7 million estimated hard-core addicts we now have, buying an estimated 80 percent of hard drugs. Were there any executions? Yes, during the three years of anti narcotics campaigning there were a total of 27 executions of dealers—clearly not the reason for their success.

Japanese Cure

The Japanese drug problem was at its height in 1963 when they decided to follow the Chinese approach and passed a drug law that included mandatory commitment of drug buyers to mental hospitals. This was accompanied by a Chinese-style propaganda campaign vilifying drug users as the destroyers of a safe sane society, making it the duty of each community to aid in the identification and rehabilitation of its own users. In less than three years the Japanese were as victorious as the Chinese. In a study of Japan's success,

Masamutsu Nagahama, chief of the Narcotics Section, Ministry of Health and Welfare said, "In conclusion, we think we can state that the drug problem is under control thanks to the strong line taken to eradicate *addiction*."

My first thought after reading the Chinese and Japanese solutions was that, if we had had an Americanized version of what these two ancient cultures did instead of our war on drugs, my brother and son would be alive today, as would the millions who have already perished during this longest war in American history.

Implications of Chinese and Japanese Solutions in America

Having grown up in the South Bronx in the fifties, it occurred to me that the image of the heroin addict during those innocent years in the US was quite similar to the socially unacceptable image projected by both the Chinese and Japanese during their successful cures. A fifties American addict was a lowlife and a felon, something despicable that lay in your hallway urinating on himself. An image that was very affective in keeping city kids off drugs. Not very PC was it? I know, I was one of those kids. It was certainly a far cry from the image of today's addict which includes super models, athletes and movie stars who do Partnership for a Drug Free America "say no" television ads between arrests and visits to the Betty Ford Clinic.

As the sixties rolled in, the image of the addict began to change. The learned among us suddenly understood how unhappiness or a dysfunctional family life could lead a poor hapless person to lose his will to say "No" and become a victim of drugs. My baby brother fell for the hype at age 15 and paid for it with 19 years of heroin addiction and ultimately suicide.

I've rarely heard an addict explain why he started on hard drugs, without reciting, parrot-like, all the psychological and socioeconomic reasons heard on national television and radio shows. It was either the Medellin Cartel, Manny Noriega, their poor economic condition, their too affluent economic condition, corrupt police, or their father's fault. And if you don't believe them, just read the news.

The image sold us of today's addict, a victim of drugs, a person of no willpower who if confronted with the presence of drugs *must* take them, is as damaging to the addict himself as it is to his community. Has the Medellin Cartel really victimized us as New York's Mayor Edward Koch once indicated in national headlines when he actually called for the retaliatory bombing of Colombia, or are our drug related problems really the fault of a flawed policy that tells us it is our government's responsibility to stop the flow of drugs or else we become hapless victims?

According to most psychologists—the "stop the drugs" philosophy could not be more damaging to those at risk. It is called enabling. The message we should be giving our children is that no matter how many illegal drugs are available, they have the will to refuse. It is a choice. By placing personal responsibility back on the users, our society is primed for a new solution to this deadly problem.

The Idea of Fight Back Is Born

Drugs are a business like any other. The American way in business competition is to focus on demand. Supply follows demand, not vice versa as our bureaucrats would have us believe. Discourage buyers and the dealers go out of business.

Throughout my career I had observed that wherever there was an obvious police presence, no matter how bad the community, drug buyers would vanish like smoke on a windy day. If the police presence was maintained long enough, dealers would shut down and move on. Suppliers and dealers, on the other hand, protected by high priced lawyers and enticed by huge and growing profits, were impossible to frighten away. If we in America could find a way to focus all our enforcement and rehabilitation resources on the buyer in an American style cure, I believed the battle would be won as quickly as happened in both Japan and China.

I found evidence all over the country, of individual communities whose aggressively vocal and visible presence on the street going after "johns" to combat prostitution was 100 percent effective, why not drugs too? I looked further and actually did find communities who, without funding or police support, were effective in stopping drug trafficking by frightening away the buyers.

Buyers, 85% of whom are so-called casual users with jobs, homes and families to protect, are frightened by almost anything. If they spot a police car, a camera, someone who even looks like a cop, an angry citizen staring at them, they would move on. Hard-core buyers, most of whom live from fix to fix, are terrified of losing their drugs to police seizures. Many are fugitives and repeat offenders from numerous drug related crimes and live in fear of being identified.

If an area was considered "hot" by the buyer—watched by the police—drug business would die instantly. I therefore began the Fight Back plan by listing various step-by-step tactics that citizens, working in partnership with police, might use to create a zone that is hostile for drug buyers.

Sure, they would move elsewhere, but it would disrupt the business entirely, which always acts to lessen all drug related crime. What would happen if the national focus of all those billions of dollars were on illegal drug buyers? There would be no "elsewhere."

Targeting Buyers and the Constitution

Among the early, unfounded fears expressed about the Fight Back program was that it might be unconstitutional. On the contrary, among the plan's primary intentions was the rescuing of our already drug-war shredded constitutional protections against illegal search and seizure, violations of privacy without due process, the taking of citizens' lives by police in violation of the rules of engagement and punishment that is disproportionate to the crime committed.

A poll taken during the Bush administration indicating that sixty percent of Americans were willing to give up rights under the Constitution to win our supply side drug war, gave government a mandate to take those rights. As a federal narcotic agent and now a defense consultant and expert witness, I am a firsthand witness to the myriad of constitutional abuses committed in the name of the drug war.

Another concern expressed was that it seemed unfair to target the "little guy"; that is the drug consumer. My answer to this is that if you had seen the amount of damage done to communities where I lived and worked by those dollars deposited there by the "little guy" you might think differently. Their dollars buy the bullets that kill kids only feet from where they satisfy their need for illegal drugs. As painful as it is for those of us who have loved ones who are drug buyers, we must recognize that it is their dollars that fuel the entire world drug economy. A high percentage of all crime, including the majority of national homicides, are drug related.

Would we fill the jails with consumers? Absolutely not. "Targeting Buyers" means dissuading the majority of them from buying illegal drugs by any legal means, with jail as a last resort. Jail terms for most buyers, with the exception of violent criminals, is neither desirable nor necessary. In fact, if we changed our focus from supply to illegal drug buyers, there would instantly be a drastic reduction in jail populations.

The reduced market would mean that far few dealers would be arrested. And most illegal drug buyers would not have to be processed through the courts at all. A non violent buyer can be handled non-criminally—a large fine and/or seizure of his vehicle. Violent and/or armed offenders caught with drugs—like the man who killed three people including my son—would be prosecuted for possession and placed in jail where they cannot continue to damage those innocents around them. Hard-core addicts with long arrest records for non-violent crimes in support of their habit, will be offered mandatory treatment in lieu of jail; that is they will be given the opportunity to get off hard drugs, or, face jail for the crime they had committed. And they might even learn a productive trade in the process. We could save their lives whether they liked it or not.

The 109th Street Experiment

As a DEA supervisory agent assigned to New York City, I was in a perfect position to isolate one of the worst, drug infested streets in our nation and run a field test to ascertain whether simply changing the enforcement focus from dealers to buyers would work as effectively as I had theorized. In March of 1989, two years before my retirement, a typical *New York Times* drug war article aimed me at Fight Back's first field test.

The article called the area of 109th Street between Amsterdam and Colombus Avenue the worst drug dealing block in the city, complete with murdcrous drug gangs and multiple crack houses. Thousands of dealer arrests had been made in the area over a several ear period yet the drug business had never been healthier.

With a 12 to 15 man squad, I planned to target the area's buyers exclusively and for the time being, to leave the dealers alone. I knew I didn't have a chance approaching US Attorney, Rudolph Giuliani for authorization for the operation. At the time, the smallest seizure case the federal court would accept was one kilo of cocaine—typical of our get the dealer policy.

Instead I contacted Manhattan Special Prosecutor Sterling Johnson, who has since been named a federal judge. His first thought was that I wanted to arrest drug consumers and prosecute them in the already clogged Manhattan Criminal Court system. I explained that my intention was merely to frighten the buyers with an arrest but not follow through with a prosecution unless the person detained was a violent criminal. I wanted to see what effect simply frightening the buyer would have on this worst of all drug dealing blocks in Manhattan. Prosecutor Johnson authorized the operation.

For the next several weeks my squad set up an ambush of drug buyers at the most active dealing location on the block, a two-sided basement. Every night a line of cars double-parked in front of the location backed up at times half way down the block, with customers running in and out making buys of cocaine, crack and heroin. As buyers would drive off, we performed a classic "angling off" operation. We followed them a distance away from the dealer, pulled them over, searched their cars and arrested them.

Most turned out to be white professionals— teachers, lawyers, salesmen, stock brokers, etc.— from outside the community as far away as Massachusetts. Most were completely bowled over by the experience of the arrest, pleading for a second chance, terrified of being exposed. All signed statements identifying the dealers in the basement. Most were eventually released with the warning that, from then on, all buyers coming onto that block would be arrested. My hope was that they would pass the word on to others. The few exceptions who were jailed were hard-core addicts with long criminal records some of whom were armed fugitives. What was apparent was that if the vast majority of these buyers had thought that there was even a possibility of arrest or identification they never would have been out there buying illegal drugs in the first place.

For the next several days we continued "angling off" buyers, identifying more dealers, collecting more statements and descriptions, spreading the words that buyers were being targeted. The operation continued from March 23 - March 30, 1989, during which time *all* drug business in the neighborhood—about two square blocks—was reduced to a trickle. It was an unusual scene for us. Dealers, for the first time, came out of the basement and stood right in front of us peering up and down the streets wondering what could have possibly happened to their customers.

On the night of March 30, armed with search and arrest warrants for the dealers we raided the basement and found it completely abandoned. Of course they had probably moved their operation to another location with less "heat," but what if this were a national policy, instead of the "stop drugs and dealers" policy that had failed for three decades? Surprisingly it was well over a year before the drug business began trickling back into the neighborhood, at nowhere near the prior levels, since buyers were still largely frightened. I was certain that if we had been able to keep the "heat" on the buyers using a trained citizens' group, the neighborhood would have remained drug free.

Thus, I began writing Fight Back, the detailed, step-by-step fight plan for communities and police to maintain a permanent street pressure on demand. Of course nothing could be guaranteed, but, living in a nation where the drug economy was causing war-like casualties on our streets and where everything else seemed doomed to failure, it certainly seemed worth a try.

Fight Back Plan of Action (short outline version):

1. Education of Community and Police to the realities of supply and demand in the drug business, to counter three decades of media and bureaucracy selling of a supply-side drug war as the "Holy Grail." This should include a community media campaign.

2. Community members are trained by police to identify drug dealing locations in their midst and, remaining in radio contact with police, become a visible deterrent to drug consumers entering their community.

3. Buyers of illegal drugs would be warned by signs and large placards that it is *they* who are targeted. They would be reminded that it is their money that attracts dealers and buys the bullets that kill the children in the community; that if they did not heed the warning, they will be arrested for possession of drugs by police, now secretly surveilling their market place and that it is they who will end up testifying against the dealer who sells them drugs.

4. Community members will be trained in other visible deterrent methods, such as bullhorns, spotlights, video-cameras, etc., and other techniques as listed in *Fight Back*— same types of methods now being used effectively by communities against prostitution "johns"—to create a "circle of fear" that will, as experience has proven, frighten away most drug buyers.

5.Plainclothes police, with community participation as spotters, begin on a selective basis to actually confront buyers, seizing drugs and ticketing those with no record of violence for future court appearances and fines. A very few actions like this will be necessary to give "teeth" to the community presence deterrent effect.

6.Community courts and prosecutors will work with the Fight Back program. The projections indicate that such a program will lessen court loads substantially. Community members will be encouraged to be present at all proceedings that affect community safety.

7.Mandatory treatment centers will be set up as an alternative to jail sentences for non-violent, crime-committing hard-core addicts where vocational training and education would be provided. The addict will be allowed to plead guilty to the crime and released into treatment with the understanding that if he returns to hard drugs, he will finish his full sentence.

8. Politically, the community would only vote for those politicians supporting a Fight Back type program.

9. Neighboring communities will join together in the program, policing each other's neighborhoods, in many cases crossing racial lines and knocking down old barriers of misunderstanding.

10. Police-Community partnership will be set up in such a way as to make police corruption and

brutality all but impossible. Police will work the community as partners, not an invading force, as is typical today.

Greenville Mississippi

In 1992, a short time after *Fight Back* was published, Sergeant Kirby Slaton of the Greenville Mississippi Police Department contacted me. Greenville, a small city on the banks of the Mississippi River, had the third highest crime rate in the South and most of it was drug related. Businesses were closing down and moving elsewhere. More and more citizens were buying and carrying guns to protect their homes and families.

Sergeant Slaton and his new chief of police, desperate for a solution, wanted to give Fight Back a try. Would I be willing to come down and help start the program?

A couple of weeks later I was in Greenville speaking to various groups of local citizens. They loved the idea, wanted to get started as soon as possible. I next spoke at all the inner city high schools, the epicenter of the problem, telling the kids that from that moment on they could look forward to their community video-taping them as they bought illegal drugs. I warned that the police would be setting traps to catch drug buyers and that by spending their money buying dope, they were paying for the very bullets that killed their little brothers and sisters.

The first reports from street informants indicated that the threat alone had made the buyers paranoid, seeing people behind every window video-taping them. The drug business had all but disappeared from the streets.

When Sergeant Slaton took me to the airport a week later, I thought this was the beginning of a change in drug war focus that would finally make an impact. Citizens were volunteering in droves and the police were gearing up to train them as their partners. A community Fight Back video was made and distributed. The effects were already seen on every corner in Greenville.

Weeks later I was shocked to hear that Sergeant Slaton was about to resign. The Justice Department was pressuring Greenville to end or alter the Fight Back program to be more "get the dealer" oriented. The community's "interference" had interrupted "important" federal investigations of dealers. By the citizen volunteers interrupting the dealers' business on the streets, the feds couldn't get enough Probable Cause to arrest them. The police finally surrendered to federal and political pressure to change Fight Back to a "drop a dime on the dealer" type program. The Fight Back citizens group was now like any other citizens group in the country. Their energy and focus was again aimed at reporting dealers to the police and having no effect whatsoever on the drug business in their midst.

Another citizens group that started a Fight Back style program in Natchez, Mississippi suffered a similar fate. One in Sacramento was met with outright antagonism by police and federal officials. It became clear that a Fight Back type program was threatening to the myriad of bureaucracies that depended on their funding for a continued, no-change war on dealers and supply. It seemed that the Fight Back program was doomed to disappear—it was simply too effective.

Cape Cod Experiment

In January, 1992, a month after my son, NYPD Sergeant Keith Richard Levine became the third man in New York City to be killed by a crack addict during the commission of a robbery, I was contacted by Sheriff Jack Demillo of Cape Cod. the sheriff, a Vietnam veteran and clinical psychologist, had studied the program and was enthusiastic about its new, common sense approach. He wanted to hire me as his Drug Information Bureau Director, in an effort to begin the program under his jurisdiction. I would later be referred to by the Massachusetts press as Cape Cod's "Drug Czar."

My job was similar to that of all the federal drug czars in that it gave me no police powers. The Fight Back Program required a full partnership between police and community to succeed. After a year of solid effort I was unable to get any police cooperation whatsoever. In fact, DEA agents who were aware of the program, confided to me that pressure was being brought to bear on police *not* to cooperate. Just as happened in Greenville, local police were told by the Justice Department and state police, that the citizens' involvement would "interfere" with drug dealer investigations. Ironic, but true. Fight Back, if it worked, would so damage the dealers' business that the feds and locals could not arrest them for drug dealing, they would simply close down.

I was successful in getting wide-spread involvement of the community, building an organization that was ready to go into action, training many of the members myself, designing a visible logo, T-shirts, hats, setting up a headquarters with telecommunications and faxes enabling instant communications with local police, yet not a single police agency would work with the citizens.

I also tried in every way to obtain the local Partnership for a Drug Free America's support to at least get a trial run of this promising program. They had the political and police connections necessary to bring it together. I was totally unsuccessful. Then in ironic twist of fate, I was accidentally put on the distribution list for one of the Partnership's in-house memos reporting on the minutes of a meeting as follows: "Meeting began with a discussion of the Fight Back Program. Both pro and con thoughts were expressed including that 'If Fight Back is successful; it could take the wind out of the sails of the Partnership." Their real concern was the same as that of all the other drug war funded bureaucracies: that the Fight Back program might put them out of business.

Of course I never did get their support and soon resigned from my position. My unfortunate experience with the Fight Back Program has not changed to date. It seems that it threatens too many vested interests, from law enforcement bureaucracies and federally funded rehabilitation Programs to covert agencies and drug education programs, for it ever to get a fair trial.

It is too easy for our bureaucrats and media to refuse to look at the methodology behind China's unparalleled and rapid success in ending a drug addiction problem many times worse than ours. But it must be mentioned here that one of the greatest influences on American war strategy was the Chinese military strategist, Sun Tzu, whose *The Art of War*, written an estimated 3500 years ago, is still studied at West Point. As Sun Tzu pointed out: "there has never been a protracted war from which a country has benefited."

Perhaps our nation has finally suffered enough under the yoke of its longest, costliest and deadliest war in history, and is ready with the coming millennium to try a new idea. Call Fight Back heresy if you wish, but it can only do better than the current failed war on drugs.

APPENDIX B

THE RAPID DRUG TEST SYSTEMS PROGRAMS

The Rapid Drug Test Systems Business Opportunities

The book you have just read underscores the fact that the drug and alcohol testing industry is in dire need of properly certified, ethical business owners. Mike Bonventre believes that this is the perfect time to start a drug and alcohol testing business. Just like millionaires were made in the Great Depression, this is the time for honest, hard-working ethical people to invest in this flourishing industry.

Rapid Drug Test Systems owes its success, in large part, to the fact that it qualifies its clients by the integrity of the programs they choose to run rather than the income stream they generate.

While it seems that everyone is looking for loopholes and shortcuts, and the industry has been flooded with online and poorly certified collectors, this works to your advantage. Mike hears from hundreds of people who cannot find a certified, qualified collector who can do a good job.

For this reason, Rapid Drug Test Systems has developed its business opportunity program.

If you see yourself in one of the following three categories, Rapid Drug Test Systems has a business plan that will certainly fit your needs:

*A current Drug & Alcohol collection facility in need of a boost;

*An experienced business owner looking for a new industry;

*A 1st time business owner with no prior business experience.

Mike Bonventre has helped many people successfully launch their business. Hear what some
of them have to say:

1. I just wanted to let you know how impressed
    I was with the professionalism you exhib-
    ited during your certification program.
    Likewise, the personal interest you have
    shown in assisting me to establish a success-
    ful drug and alcohol test collection busi-
    ness has far exceeded my expectations.
    As a former law enforcement officer and
    polygraph examiner, it was important to
    me that I be certified by an organization
    with integrity. Your genuine desire to pro-
    mote and raise industry standards speaks
    volumes for the integrity of your program.
    You most certainly are the mentor I had
    hoped for!

    ... Jack Sparagowski, Reliable Drug Testing
    Inc. Sylvania, Ohio

2. I have hired Michael Bonventre on sev-
    eral occasions as a consultant to certify
    myself and my employees in the DOT

CFR 49 Part 40 rules and regulations for drug and alcohol collections. Michael was extremely knowledgeable in both these fields because he is also a collector of these services. He explained things well, we had hands on training and had several different examples presented to us about the collection process. His training tools were modern and his information and booklets had updated materials. I would recommend hiring Michael for consulting and training of any staff members on the proper techniques and rules and regulations of the drug and alcohol DOT procedures.

… Nancy Sucharski, Industrial Med Testing
Plattsburgh, New York

Call Mike Bonventre today at (607-687-7612) to discuss how you can join this dynamic industry or visit the

Rapid Drug Test Systems Website (www.rapid-drugtest.com) to learn more about your future.

The Rapid Drug Test Systems

CFR 49 Part 40 Certification & Train The Trainer Course

Rapid Drug Test Systems has provided hundreds of CFR 49 Part 40 Drug and Alcohol certifications for some of the nation's largest medical facilities, clinics, third party administrators and private collection businesses.

Whether you are being certified for the first time, or you realize that you have been inadequately prepared by mass certification training mills or on line trainings, RDTS will be the only training required for you to start or move on with complete confidence. You will perform the five specific mock collections required by the CFR personally monitored by a qualified collector who has demonstrated the necessary knowledge, skills and abilities outlined in the CFR's. This is something no online or mass certification trainer offers. You will receive the RDTS user-friendly training manual which will become your easy reference handbook in the field. All of this is offered in the relaxed, comfortable setting at

Rapid Drug Test Systems Corporate Offices in upstate New York or, if you prefer, at your facility.

Even the best trained and experienced collectors need occasional help. RDTS stays with its trainees offering ongoing phone support that does not require spending additional dollars. RDTS certified collectors receive one full year of phone support which is included in the cost of the training. And since drug and alcohol testing is not a nine to five job, the phone support is offered 24/7 by Mike Bonventre, personally. No other training program offers this unique and invaluable feature.

Listen to what a seasoned collector said about an RDTS refresher course:

Hi Mike,

Thank you for sharing a copy of your service agreement, it looks great. I want to thank you VERY much for sharing your time and expertise, along with the good meals and the use of your car. It was an outstanding refresher course! You made everything concise, relevant and pertinent. You even taught this old collector some new procedures. It was well worth the trip to New

York to take a course from you. My friends can't believe that you even provided airport transportation. Thank you for your hospitality. It was a pleasure to meet you and hear your fascinating stories. You are a rare individual with a big heart. Stop by if you're ever in California

(the rural Northern part). Otherwise, I'll see you in five years. Thanks again.

Sincerely, Mae Linn Brooks
North Bay Corporate Health Services
Santa Rosa, CA.

Call Mike Bonventre (607-687-7612) or visit at www.rapiddrugtest.com for more information on the training programs.

The Rapid Drug Test Systems
Family and Youth Initiative Program

(FYI)

RDTS provides consulting for families. We are seeing an alarming growth in young drug addicts often starting in middle school. As discussed in the book, there are very few programs that provide realistic preventative treatment for our youth.

Law enforcement, rehab and medical facilities are equipped and funded to counsel and treat addicts. RDTS-FYI program extends its expertise to parents and children before they become fully engulfed in the world of drugs and addiction.

The FYI program teaches parents how to rec-ognize the warning signs. Parents and children learn how to communicate their fears and con-cerns to each other. For those families and chil-dren who are already immersed in the system as a result of active addiction, FYI offers post reha-bilitation consultation. A complementary pro-gram that is a part of helping families and youths is the Fight Back program. This program helps families and neighborhoods groups clean up their neighborhoods from the scourge of drug traffic, gangs and crime.

RDTS-FYI and "Fight Back" consulting has one simple strategy… to help families and commu-nities help themselves. If you have pre or post addiction concerns or need help with drugs, gangs or crime in your community.

Call Mike Bonventre (607-687-7612) or visit at www.rapiddrugtest.com for more information on eradicating drug traffic and drug related crime in your community.

Made in the USA
San Bernardino, CA
02 October 2013